The Little Book of Peace

The Little Book of Peace

EDITED BY
PATRICIA J. CHUI

THE LYONS PRESS
Guilford, Connecticut

An imprint of The Globe Pequot Press

The Lyons Press is an imprint of the Globe Pequot Press.

First Lyons Press edition, November 2001

Printed in Canada

ISBN 1-58574-570-7

Library of Congress Cataloging-in-Publication Data is available on file.

For the victims of September 11

Contents

Introduction

When terrorists attacked the World Trade Center and the Pentagon on September 11, 2001, I was overseas on vacation. Four days later, in a cab from LAX, I looked out the window and was moved almost to tears by the countless American flags flying from cars and buildings. My cabdriver, on the other hand, seemed agitated. "I'm just so mad at those idiots," he said, knocking me out of my reverie. "I hope by Monday we'll have obliterated Afghanistan and Palestine."

Today, those flags no longer move me; they signify something different. A little over a week ago, the U.S. government began bombing targets in Afghanistan, kicking off its protracted "war against terrorism" in retaliation for the September 11 attacks. We are a nation at war, and the thought of it—the *fact* of it—fills me with dread, not only at what is happening now but also at what may come next. Yet at the same time, I find that it hasn't been so easy to condemn all those who do support military action. If I say I want peace instead of war, what does that mean? Does it mean we should do nothing? It seems pretty easy in the abstract to shout, *"What do we want? Peace! When do we want it? Now!"* What isn't so easy is the reality of over 5,000 people being killed in a single morning, a skyline forever altered, and a country living in fear. Given all that, how can we turn the other cheek?

As the quotations in this book prove, peace doesn't mean doing nothing, and pacifism is rarely easy. The people quoted here are writers, philosophers, scientists, and statesmen; they are religious and secular, young and old, hopeful and jaded. Like the rest of us, they have struggled to understand what peace is and how to find it (or, in some cases, whether they even want it). And while they may not claim to have all the answers, it's the asking that yields the most provocative fruit. They find that peace is justice, not revenge. It comes from small gestures and bold policies. It takes courage and faith. It's the result of hard work, dialogue, and rejection of hate. Ultimately, though, what I think these quotations demonstrate is that attaining peace is an ideal: In many ways, it's the journey there that counts.

So it seems, in the end, that peace is just as difficult as war; but, if anything, it's that very complexity that should make us appreciate it all the more. No matter how complicated the ideal may be, I still believe that, in the words of Walt Whitman, "Peace is always beautiful." And therefore, be you pacifist, war supporter, or something in between, I wish you strength on your journey. Peace be with you.

—Patricia J. Chui
Brooklyn, New York
October 16, 2001

The Little Book of Peace

Give peace in our time, O Lord.

—*THE BOOK OF COMMON PRAYER*

Ah, when shall all men's good
Be each man's rule, and universal peace
Lie like a shaft of light across the land,
And like a lane of beams athwart the sea,
Thro' all the circle of the golden year?

—ALFRED TENNYSON, "THE GOLDEN YEAR" (1842)

A peace above all earthly dignities,
A still and quiet conscience.

—WILLIAM SHAKESPEARE, *KING HENRY VIII*

What is peace? Is it war? No. Is it strife? No. Is it lovely, and gentle, and beautiful, and pleasant, and serene, and joyful? O yes!

—CHARLES DICKENS, *BLEAK HOUSE* (1852–53)

Peace is freedom in tranquility.

—CICERO, *PHILIPPICAE* (44 B.C.)

Peace is a necessary condition of spirituality, no less than an inevitable result of it.

—ALDOUS HUXLEY, "SEVEN MEDITATIONS"

Whatever peace I know rests in the natural world, in feeling myself a part of it, even in a small way.
—MAY SARTON, *JOURNAL OF SOLITUDE* (1973)

I take it that what all men are really after is some form or perhaps only some formula of peace.
—JOSEPH CONRAD, *UNDER WESTERN EYES* (1911)

First keep the peace within yourself, then you can also bring peace to others.
—THOMAS À KEMPIS, *THE IMITATION OF CHRIST* (c. 1420)

And peace, which everywhere
With so much earnestness you do pursue,
Is only there.

—GEORGE HERBERT, "PEACE"

Inner peace is beyond victory or defeat.

—*BHAGAVAD GITA* (6TH CENTURY B.C.), TR.
JUAN MASCARÓ (1962)

Acquire inner peace and a multitude will find their salvation near you.

—CATHERINE DE HUECK DOHERTY, *POUSTINIA* (1975)

There is no such thing as inner peace. There is only nervousness and death.

—FRAN LEBOWITZ, *METROPOLITAN LIFE* (1978)

Looking for peace is like looking for a turtle with a mustache: you won't be able to find it. But when your heart is ready, peace will come looking for you.

—AJAHN CHAH, *REFLECTIONS* (1994)

Peace is when time doesn't matter as it passes by.

—MARIA SCHELL, IN *TIME* (MARCH 3, 1958)

Peace, peace is what I seek and public calm,
Endless extinction of unhappy hates.
—MATTHEW ARNOLD, *MEROPE* (1858)

Hate is not conquered by hate: hate is conquered
by love. This is a law eternal.
—BUDDHA, *THE DHAMMAPADA*, TR. JUAN MASCARÓ
(1973)

Five enemies of peace inhabit with us—avarice, am-
bition, envy, anger, and pride; if these were to be ban-
ished, we should infallibly enjoy perpetual peace.
—PETRARCH

We plant seeds that will flower as results in our lives, so best to remove the weeds of anger, avarice, envy and doubt, that peace and abundance may manifest for all.

—DOROTHY DAY

Our anger and annoyance are more detrimental to us than the things themselves which anger or annoy us.

—MARCUS AURELIUS, *MEDITATIONS*, TR. MAXWELL STANIFORTH (1964)

Forgo your anger for a moment and save yourself a hundred days of trouble.

—CHINESE PROVERB

It is particularly hard on us as pacifists, of course, to face our own anger. It is particularly painful for us—hard on our pride, too—to have to discover in ourselves murderers.

—BARBARA DEMING, "ON ANGER," *WE CANNOT LIVE WITHOUT OUR LIVES* (1974)

The price of hating other human beings is loving oneself less.

—ELDRIDGE CLEAVER, "ON BECOMING," *SOUL ON ICE* (1968)

He who can control his rising anger as a coachman controls his carriage at full speed, this man I call a good driver: others merely hold the reins.

—BUDDHA, *THE DHAMMAPADA*

A loving person lives in a loving world. A hostile person lives in a hostile world. Everyone you meet is your mirror.

—KEN KEYES, JR., IN *CATHOLIC DIGEST* (JUNE 2000)

Peace is not a relationship of nations. It is a condition of mind brought about by a serenity of soul. . . . Lasting peace can come only to peaceful people.

—Jawaharlal Nehru

Soft is stronger than hard, water than rock, love than violence.

—Herman Hesse, *Reflections*, ed. Volker Michels (1974)

Life appears to me too short to be spent in nursing animosity or registering wrongs.

—Charlotte Brontë, *Jane Eyre* (1847)

All that a pacifist can undertake—but it is a very great deal—is to refuse to kill, injure or otherwise cause suffering to another human creature, and untiringly to order his life by the rule of love though others may be captured by hate.

—VERA BRITTAIN, "WHAT CAN WE DO IN WARTIME?" IN *FORWARD* (SEPTEMBER 19, 1939)

Whosoever shall smite thee on thy right cheek, turn to him the other also.

—*BIBLE*, MATTHEW 5:39

Instead of killing and dying in order to produce the being that we are not, we have to live and let live in order to create what we are.

—ALBERT CAMUS, *THE REBEL* (1951)

We are not going to be able to operate our space-ship earth successfully nor for much longer unless we see it as a whole spaceship and our fate as common. It has to be everybody or nobody.

—R. BUCKMINSTER FULLER, *OPERATING MANUAL FOR SPACESHIP EARTH* (1969)

We can find common ground only by moving to higher ground.

— JIM WALLIS, *THE SOUL OF POLITICS* (1994)

High above hate I dwell:
O storms! farewell.

— LOUISE IMOGEN GUINEY, "THE SANCTUARY," *THE MARTYRS' IDYL* (1899)

Where there is discord, may we bring harmony. Where there is error may we bring truth. Where there is doubt may we bring faith. Where there is despair may we bring hope.

—MARGARET THATCHER, ON THE STEPS OF 10 DOWNING STREET (MAY 1979), AFTER HER FIRST ELECTION VICTORY

Lord, make me an instrument of Your peace!
Where there is hatred let me sow love;
Where there is injury, pardon.

—SAINT FRANCIS OF ASSISI, "PRAYER OF ST. FRANCIS"

Did St. Francis preach to the birds? Whatever for? If he really liked birds he would have done better to preach to cats.

—REBECCA WEST, *THIS REAL NIGHT* (1985)

If you want to make peace, you don't talk to your friends. You talk to your enemies.

—MOSHE DAYAN, IN *NEWSWEEK* (October 17, 1977)

The best preparedness is the one that disarms the hostility of other nations and makes friends of them.

—HELEN KELLER

I destroy my enemies when I make them my friends.

—ABRAHAM LINCOLN

We have learned the simple truth, as Emerson said, that the only way to have a friend is to be one. We can gain no lasting peace if we approach it with suspicion or mistrust or with fear.

—FRANKLIN DELANO ROOSEVELT, FOURTH INAUGURAL ADDRESS (JANUARY 20, 1945)

Peace is not made with friends. Peace is made with enemies.

—YITZHAK RABIN, *NEW YORK TIMES* (SEPTEMBER 5, 1993)

If you want to make peace with your enemy, you have to work with your enemy. Then he becomes your partner.

—NELSON MANDELA, *LONG WALK TO FREEDOM* (1994)

Always forgive your enemies. Nothing annoys them more.

—OSCAR WILDE

Can I see another's woe,
And not be in sorrow too?
Can I see another's grief,
And not seek for kind relief?

—WILLIAM BLAKE, "ON ANOTHER'S SORROW," *SONGS OF INNOCENCE* (1789)

If we have no peace, it is because we have forgotten that we belong to each other.

—MOTHER TERESA OF CALCUTTA

We need to dissolve the lie that some people have a right to think of other people as their property. And we need at last to form . . . a circle that includes us all, in which all of us are seen as equal.

—BARBARA DEMING, LECTURE AT FLORIDA STATE UNIVERSITY (MARCH 4, 1977)

No man is an island, entire of itself; every man is a piece of the continent . . . any man's death diminishes me, because I am involved in mankind; and therefore never send to know for whom the bell tolls; it tolls for thee.

—JOHN DONNE, *DEVOTIONS UPON EMERGENT OCCASIONS* (1624)

States are more like people than they are like anything else: they exist by purpose, reason, suffering, and joy. And peace between states is also like peace between people. It involves the willing renunciation of purpose, in the mutual desire not to do, but to be.

—ROGER SCRUTON, "IMPOSSIBLE PARTNERS," *UNTIMELY TRACTS* (1987)

If there is to be any peace it will come through being, not having.

> —HENRY MILLER, "THE WISDOM OF THE HEART," *THE WISDOM OF THE HEART* (1941)

All the nations and peoples are too closely knit together today for any one of them to imagine that it can live apart. Peace has been said to be indivisible, so is freedom, so is prosperity now, and so also is disaster in this one world that can no longer be split into isolated fragments.

> —JAWAHARLAL NEHRU, "AWAKE TO FREEDOM," SPEECH TO THE CONSTITUENT ASSEMBLY, NEW DELHI (AUGUST 14, 1947)

It is thus tolerance that is the source of peace, and intolerance that is the source of disorder and squabbling.

—PIERRE BAYLE, *PHILOSOPHICAL COMMENTARY ON THE WORDS "COMPEL THEM TO COME IN,"* ED. JEAN-MICHEL GROS (1686)

———

There is a certain kind of peace that is not merely the absence of war. It is larger than that. . . . The peace I am thinking of is the dance of an open mind when it engages another equally open one.

—TONI MORRISON, *THE DANCING MIND* (1996)

A strong nation, like a strong person, can afford to be gentle, firm, thoughtful, and restrained. It can afford to extend a helping hand to others. It's a weak nation, like a weak person, that must behave with bluster and boasting and rashness and other signs of insecurity.

—JIMMY CARTER, SPEECH AT LIBERTY PARTY DINNER, NEW YORK CITY (OCTOBER 14, 1976)

When you're finally up on the moon, looking back at the earth, all these differences and nationalistic traits are pretty well going to blend and you're going to get a concept that maybe this is really one world and why the hell can't we learn to live together like decent people?

—FRANK BORMAN

The wise man belongs to all countries, for the home of a great soul is the whole world.

—DEMOCRITUS, IN KARL R. POPPER, *THE OPEN SOCIETY AND ITS ENEMIES* (1945)

———— ◆•◆•◆ ————

The basis of world peace is the teaching which runs through almost all the great religions of the world. "Love thy neighbor as thyself." Christ, some of the other great Jewish teachers, Buddha, all preached it. Their followers forgot it.

—ELEANOR ROOSEVELT (1925), IN JOSEPH P. LASH, *ELEANOR AND FRANKLIN* (1971)

Mankind must remember that peace is not God's gift to his creatures; peace is our gift to each other.

—ELIE WIESEL, NOBEL PEACE PRIZE ACCEPTANCE LECTURE, OSLO (DECEMBER 11, 1986)

The social progress, order, security and peace of each country are necessarily connected with the social progress, order, security and peace of all other countries.

—POPE JOHN XXIII, *PACEM IN TERRIS* (April 11, 1963)

The progress of freedom depends more upon the maintenance of peace, the spread of commerce, and the diffusion of education, than upon the labours of cabinets and foreign offices.

—RICHARD COBDEN, SPEECH TO THE HOUSE OF COMMONS (JUNE 26, 1850)

Peace does not rest in charters and covenants alone. It lies in the hearts and minds of the people.

—JOHN FITZGERALD KENNEDY, ADDRESS TO THE UNITED NATIONS, NEW YORK CITY (SEPTEMBER 20, 1963)

Love is not a doctrine. Peace is not an international agreement. Love and Peace are beings who live as possibilities in us.

—MARY CAROLINE RICHARDS, *CENTERING* (1964)

———◆◆◆———

There never was a war that was not inward; I must fight till I have conquered in myself what causes war.

—MARIANNE MOORE, "IN DISTRUST OF MERITS," *NEVERTHELESS* (1944)

Ultimately, we have just one moral duty: to reclaim large areas of peace in ourselves, more and more peace, and to reflect it towards others. And the more peace there is in us, the more peace there will also be in our troubled world.

—ETTY HILLESUM (1942), *AN INTERRUPTED LIFE: THE DIARIES, 1941–1943, AND LETTERS FROM WESTERBROOK* (1983)

———◦•◦•◦———

We used to wonder where war lived, what it was that made it so vile. And now we realize that we know where it lives, that it is inside ourselves.

—ALBERT CAMUS, *NOTEBOOKS*, VOL. 3 (1966), ENTRY FOR SEPTEMBER 7, 1939

Men are at war with each other because each man is at war with himself.

—FRANCIS MEEHAN

<hr />

All your strength is in your union.
All your danger is in discord;
Therefore be at peace henceforward,
And as brothers live together.

—HENRY WADSWORTH LONGFELLOW, THE SONG OF HIAWATHA (1855)

<hr />

Peace is achieved one person at a time, through a series of friendships.

—FATMA REDA, IN THE MINNESOTA WOMEN'S PRESS (1991)

We are members one of another; so that you cannot injure or help your neighbor without injuring or helping yourself.

—GEORGE BERNARD SHAW, *ANDROCLES AND THE LION* (1912)

One little person, giving all of her time to peace, makes news. Many people, giving some of their time, can make history.

—PEACE PILGRIM

Never doubt that a small group of thoughtful committed citizens can change the world: Indeed it's the only thing that ever has.

—MARGARET MEAD

———◆•◆•◆———

My humanity is bound up in yours, for we can only be human together.

—ARCHBISHOP DESMOND TUTU

———◆•◆•◆———

I am not an Athenian or a Greek, but a citizen of the world.

—SOCRATES, FROM PLUTARCH, *OF BANISHMENT*

Without free, self-respecting, and autonomous citizens there can be no free and independent nations. Without internal peace, that is, peace among citizens and between the citizens and the state, there can be no guarantee of external peace.

—VÁCLAV HAVEL, *LIVING IN TRUTH* (1986)

Peace, like charity, begins at home.

—FRANKLIN DELANO ROOSEVELT, SPEECH IN CHATAQUA, NEW YORK (AUGUST 14, 1936)

Thaw with his gentle persuasion is more powerful than Thor with his hammer. The one melts, the other but breaks in pieces.

—HENRY DAVID THOREAU, *WALDEN* (1854)

Much violence is based on the illusion that life is a property to be defended and not to be shared.

—HENRI NOUWEN

They pass peaceful lives who ignore *mine* and *thine*.

—PUBLIUS SYRUS, *MORAL SAYINGS*, TR. DARIUS LYMAN, JR. (1862)

Peace is no more than a dream as long as we need the comfort of the clan.

—PETER NICHOLS, IN THE *LONDON INDEPENDENT* (SEPTEMBER 1, 1990)

There is only one way of not hating those who do us wrong, and that is by doing them good.

—HENRI AMIEL, JOURNAL (NOVEMBER 22, 1880), TR. MRS. HUMPHREY WARD (1887)

I would permit no man . . . to narrow and degrade my soul by making me hate him.

—BOOKER T. WASHINGTON, *UP FROM SLAVERY* (1901)

The love of one's country is a natural thing. But why should love stop at the border?

—PABLO CASALS, *JOYS AND SORROWS: REFLECTIONS BY PABLO CASALS* (1970)

The prophecy of a world moving toward political unity is the light which guides all that is best, most vigorous, most truly alive in the work of our time. It gives sense to what we are doing. Nothing else does.

—WALTER LIPPMAN, "REFLECTION AFTER ARMISTICE DAY," *NEW YORK HERALD TRIBUNE* (NOVEMBER 12, 1931)

I love my country very much. But I must say I love people all over the world, and we better all start loving each other or we're going to blow each other to kingdom come.

—TED TURNER

You cannot shake hands with a clenched fist.

—INDIRA GANDHI, PRESS CONFERENCE, NEW DELHI
(OCTOBER 19, 1971)

We can no longer afford to worship the god of hate or bow before the altar of retaliation.

—MARTIN LUTHER KING, JR., "BEYOND VIETNAM,"
SPEECH AT RIVERSIDE CHURCH, NEW YORK CITY
(APRIL 4, 1967)

You may call for peace as loudly as you wish, but where there is no brotherhood there can in the end be no peace.

> —MAX LERNER, "THE GIFTS OF THE MAGI," *ACTIONS AND PASSIONS* (1949)

You can't hold a man down without staying down with him.

> —BOOKER T. WASHINGTON

You can stand tall without standing on someone. You can be a victor without having victims.

> —HARRIET WOODS

No matter how big a nation is, it is no stronger than its weakest people, and as long as you keep a person down, some part of you has to be down there to hold him down, so it means you cannot soar as you might otherwise.

—MARIAN ANDERSON, CBS TELEVISION INTERVIEW
(DECEMBER 30, 1957)

Peace produced by suppression is neither natural nor desirable.

—ANNA JULIA COOPER, *A VOICE FROM THE SOUTH*,
PART 2 (1892)

The tough-minded . . . respect difference. Their goal is a world made safe for differences, where the United States may be American to the hilt without threatening the peace of the world, and France may be France, and Japan may be Japan on the same conditions.

—RUTH FULTON BENEDICT, *THE CHRYSANTHEMUM AND THE SWORD* (1946)

The most violent element in society is ignorance.

—EMMA GOLDMAN

Where they make a desert, they call it peace.

—TACITUS, *AGRICOLA* (CALGACUS, REFERRING TO THE ROMANS)

At this moment, death and life are poised as on a razor's edge. It is for us to choose what we will. Let us choose life.

—MORARJI DESAI, AT THE SPECIAL SESSION OF THE UNITED NATIONS GENERAL ASSEMBLY, NEW YORK CITY (JUNE 9, 1978)

Peace depends ultimately not on political arrangements but on the conscience of mankind.

—HENRY A. KISSINGER, "GOLDA MEIR: AN APPRECIATION" (NOVEMBER 13, 1977)

There never was a good war or a bad peace.

> —BENJAMIN FRANKLIN, LETTER TO SIR JOSEPH BANKS
> (JULY 27, 1783)

It hath been said that an unjust peace is to be pre-
ferred before a just war.

> —SAMUEL BUTLER, *BUTLER'S REMAINS, SPEECHES IN THE
> RUMP PARLIAMANT* (1759)

Wherever there is war, there must be injustice on
one side or on the other, or on both.

> —JOHN RUSKIN, *MODERN PAINTERS* (1843–60)

I cease not to advocate peace; even though unjust it is better than the most just war.

—CICERO, *EPISTOLAE AD ATTICUM*

A "just war" is hospitable to every self-deception on the part of those waging it, none more than the certainty of virtue, under whose shelter every abomination can be committed with a clear conscience.

—ALEXANDER COCKBURN, *NEW STATESMAN AND SOCIETY* (FEBRUARY 8, 1991)

What is human warfare but just this; an effort to make the laws of God and nature take sides with one party.

—HENRY DAVID THOREAU

War grows out of the desire of the individual to gain advantage at the expense of his fellow man.

—NAPOLEON HILL

We have war when at least one of the parties to a conflict wants something more than it wants peace.

—JEANNE J. KIRKPATRICK, IN *READER'S DIGEST* (1994)

War is the admission of defeat in the face of conflicting interests.

—GERMAINE GREER, "REVOLUTION," *THE FEMALE EUNUCH* (1970)

Though peace be made, yet it's interest that keeps peace.

—OLIVER CROMWELL, REFERRING TO THE SAYING AS "A MAXIM NOT TO BE DESPISED," PARLIAMENT SPEECH (SEPTEMBER 4, 1654)

Peace is a virtual, mute, sustained victory of potential powers against probable greeds.

—PAUL VALÉRY, "GREATNESS AND DECADENCE OF EUROPE," *REFLECTIONS ON THE WORLD TODAY* (1931), TR. FRANCIS SCARFE

War crushes with bloody heel all justice, all happiness, all that is Godlike in man. In our age there can be no peace that is not honorable; there can be no war that is not dishonorable.

—CHARLES SUMNER, SPEECH, "THE TRUE GRANDEUR OF NATIONS" (JULY 4, 1845)

An insincere peace is better than a sincere war.

—YIDDISH PROVERB

Those who prefer victory to peace will have neither.

—ANONYMOUS

There is such a thing as a man being too proud to fight. There is such a thing as a nation being so right that it does not need to convince others by force that it is right.

—WOODROW WILSON, SPEECH IN PHILADELPHIA (MAY 10, 1915)

Our researchers into Public Opinion are content
That he held the proper opinions for the time of year;
When there was peace, he was for peace: when there was war, he went.

—W. H. AUDEN, "THE UNKNOWN CITIZEN (TO JS/07/M/378 THIS MARBLE MONUMENT IS ERECTED BY THE STATE)," *ANOTHER TIME* (1940)

Certain peace is better and safer than anticipated victory.

—LIVY, *AB URBE CONDITA* (C. 29 B.C.)

———◆◆◆———

Better beans and bacon in peace than cakes and ale in fear.

—AESOP, "THE TOWN MOUSE AND THE COUNTRY MOUSE," *FABLES* (6th century B.C.), TR. JOSEPH JACOBS
See also Proverbs 15:17, "Better is a dinner of herbs where love is, than a stalled ox and hatred therewith."

When you're at war you think about a better life; when you're at peace you think about a more comfortable one.

——THORNTON WILDER, *THE SKIN OF OUR TEETH* (1942)

Before the war, and especially before the Boer War, it was summer all the year round.

——GEORGE ORWELL, *COMING UP FOR AIR* (1939)

An ounce of peace is worth more than a pound of victory.

——SAINT ROBERT BELLARMINE, IN POPE JOHN XIII, *JOURNAL OF A SOUL* (1964), TR. DOROTHY WHITE (1965)

It is always easier to fight for one's principles than
to live up to them.

—ALFRED ADLER, REMARK TO A FRIEND, IN PHYLLIS
BOTTOME, *ALFRED ADLER: A BIOGRAPHY* (1939)

If you like peace, don't contradict anybody.

—HUNGARIAN PROVERB

Peace demands more, not less, from a people. Peace
lacks the clarity of purpose and the cadence of war.
War is scripted: peace is improvisation.

—RICHARD M. NIXON, *BEYOND PEACE* (1994)

All men desire peace but few indeed desire those
things which make for peace.

—THOMAS À KEMPIS, *THE IMITATION OF CHRIST*
(c. 1420)

Let us not accept violence as the way of peace. Let
us instead begin by respecting true freedom: the re-
sulting peace will be able to satisfy the world's expectations, for it will be a peace built on justice, a
peace founded on the incomparable dignity of the
free human being.

—POPE JOHN PAUL II, MESSAGE FOR THE FOURTEENTH
WORLD DAY OF PEACE (JANUARY 1, 1981)

You can't separate peace from freedom because no one can be at peace unless he has his freedom.

—MALCOLM X, "PROSPECTS FOR FREEDOM IN 1965,"
SPEECH IN NEW YORK CITY (JANUARY 7, 1965)

The gentlemen may cry, Peace, peace! but there is no peace. The war has actually begun! . . . Is life so dear or peace so sweet as to be purchased at the price of chains and liberty? Forbid it, Almighty God. I know not what course others may take, but as for me, give me liberty or give me death!

—PATRICK HENRY, SPEECH IN VIRGINIA CONVENTION,
RICHMOND (MARCH 23, 1775)

We seem always ready to pay the price for war. Almost gladly we give our time and our treasures—our limbs and even our lives—for war. But we expect to get peace for nothing.

—PEACE PILGRIM, *PEACE PILGRIM: HER LIFE AND WORK IN HER OWN WORDS* (1982)

Peace, *n.* In international affairs, a period of cheating between two periods of fighting.

—AMBROSE BIERCE, *THE DEVIL'S DICTIONARY* (1911)

Peace is more important than all justice; and peace was not made for the sake of justice, but justice for the sake of peace.

—MARTIN LUTHER, *ON MARRIAGE* (1530)

Peace and justice are two sides of the same coin.

—DWIGHT D. EISENHOWER, NEWS CONFERENCE, WASHINGTON, D.C. (FEBRUARY 6, 1937)

An act of justice closes the book on a misdeed; an act of vengeance writes one of its own.

—MARILYN VOS SAVANT

An eye for an eye leaves the whole world blind.

—MOHANDAS K. GANDHI
Also cited as "An eye for an eye makes the whole world blind" or "An eye for an eye only ends up making the whole world blind."

There is no way to peace. Peace is the way.

—A. J. MUSTE, IN "DEBASING DISSENT" (EDITORIAL), *NEW YORK TIMES* (NOVEMBER 16, 1967)

When fire and water are at war, it is the fire that loses.

—SPANISH PROVERB

Accurst be he that first invented war.

—CHRISTOPHER MARLOWE, *TAMBURLAINE THE GREAT* (c. 1587)

War is not inherent in human beings. We learn war and we learn peace. The culture of peace is something which is learned, just as violence is learned and war culture is learned.

—ELISE BOULDING, KEYNOTE ADDRESS AT BOSTON RESEARCH CENTER CONFERENCE "CREATING CULTURES OF PEACE" (FEBRUARY 5, 1999)

War is an invention of the human mind. The human mind can invent peace.

—NORMAN COUSINS, *WHO SPEAKS FOR MAN?* (1953)

Since wars begin in the minds of men, it is in the minds of men that the defences of peace must be constructed.

—CONSTITUTION OF THE UNITED NATIONS EDUCATIONAL, SCIENTIFIC, AND CULTURAL ORGANIZATION (UNESCO) (1945)

Wars are not acts of God. They are caused by man, by man-made institutions, by the way in which man has organized his society. What man has made, man can change.

—FREDERICK MOORE VINSON, SPEECH AT ARLINGTON NATIONAL CEMETERY (MEMORIAL DAY, 1945)

Only through a harmonization of human wills, in a compact freely entered into in the light of divine necessity, can peace prevail among men.

—ARNOLD J. TOYNBEE, *A STUDY OF HISTORY* (1961)

"Peace upon earth!" was said. We sing it,

And pay a million priests to bring it.

After two thousand years of mass

We've got as far as poison gas.

—THOMAS HARDY, "CHRISTMAS: 1924," *WINTER WORDS IN VARIOUS MOODS AND METRES* (1928)

It is easier to make war than to make peace.

—GEORGES CLEMENCEAU, SPEECH IN VERDUN, FRANCE (JULY 20, 1919)

Making peace, I have found, is much harder than making war.

—GERRY ADAMS, TELEVISION INTERVIEW ON *CHARLIE ROSE* (FEBRUARY 2, 1994)

Indifference creates an artificial peace.

—MASON COOLEY, CITY APHORISMS, NINTH
SELECTION (1992)

———•+•+•———

Nothing contributes more to peace of soul than
having no opinion at all.

—GEORG CHRISTOPH LICHTENBERG, APHORISMS

———•+•+•———

Mutual cowardice keeps us in peace.

—SAMUEL JOHNSON, IN JAMES BOSWELL, THE LIFE OF
SAMUEL JOHNSON (1791)

The deliberate aim at Peace very easily passes into its bastard substitute, Anesthesia.

—ALFRED NORTH WHITEHEAD, *ADVENTURES OF IDEAS* (1933)

The mere absence of war is not peace.

—JOHN FITZGERALD KENNEDY, STATE OF THE UNION ADDRESS (JANUARY 14, 1963)

Peace is not an absence of war, it is a virtue, a state of mind, a disposition for benevolence, confidence, justice.

—BENEDICT SPINOZA, *THEOLOGICAL-POLITICAL TREATISE* (1670)

They have not wanted Peace at all; they have wanted to be spared war—as though the absence of war was the same as peace.

—DOROTHY THOMPSON, SYNDICATED COLUMN
"ON THE RECORD" (1958)

Because we want the peace with half a heart and half a life and will, the war, of course, continues, because the waging of war, by its nature, is total—but the waging of peace, by our own cowardice, is partial.

—DANIEL BERRIGAN, *NO BARS TO MANHOOD* (1970)

We are now suffering the evils of a long peace. Luxury, more deadly than war, broods over the city, and avenges a conquered world.

—JUVENAL, *SATIRES*

War its thousands slays, Peace, its ten thousands.

—BEILBY PORTEUS, *DEATH* (1759)

That piecemeal peace is poor peace. What pure
    peace allows
Alarms of wars, the daunting wars, the death of it?

—GERARD MANLEY HOPKINS, "PEACE" (1918)

Conflict is inevitable, but combat is optional.

> —MAX LUCADO

I want to stand by my country, but I cannot vote for war. I vote no.

> —JEANNETTE RANKIN, VOTING AGAINST DECLARATION
> OF WAR (1917), IN HANNAH JOSEPHSON, *JEANNETTE
> RANKIN* (1974)

I was struck by what one of them [the clergy] said: "As we act, let us not become the evil that we deplore."

> —BARBARA LEE, ON HER VOTE AGAINST THE USE OF
> MILITARY ACTION TO RESPOND TO THE ATTACKS ON NEW
> YORK CITY'S WORLD TRADE CENTER, "BARBARA LEE'S
> STAND," *THE NATION* (October 8, 2001)

If it were proved to me that in making war, my ideal had a chance of being realized, I would still say "No" to war. For one does not create human society on mounds of corpses.

  —LOUIS LECOIN

The sword of murder is not the balance of justice.
Blood does not wipe out dishonor,
Nor violence indicate possession.

    —JULIA WARD HOWE, MOTHER'S DAY
    PROCLAMATION (1870)

The story of the human race is characterized by efforts to get along much more than by violent disputes, although it's the latter that make the history books. Violence is actually exceptional. The human race has survived because of cooperation, not aggression.

—GERARD VANDERHAAR

The belief in the possibility of a short decisive war appears to be one of the most ancient and dangerous of human illusions.

—ROBERT LYND

But then peace, peace! I am so mistrustful of it: so much afraid that it means a sort of weakness and giving in.

—D. H. LAWRENCE, LETTER, REPRINTED IN
SELECTED LETTERS OF D. H. LAWRENCE, ED. JAMES
T. BOULTON (1997)

Only in time of fear is government thrown back to its primitive and sole function of self-defense and the many interests of which it is the guardian become subordinate to that.

—JANE ADDAMS, "WOMEN, WAR AND SUFFRAGE,"
SURVEY 6 NOVEMBER 1915

It seems to me that there are two great enemies of peace—fear and selfishness.

—KATHERINE PATERSON, IN *THE HORN BOOK* (1991)

Very few people chose war. They chose selfishness and the result was war. Each of us, individually and nationally, must choose: total love or total war.

—DAVID DELLINGER

When we say peace as a word, war
As a flare of fire leaps across our eyes.

—MURIEL RUKEYSER, "THE DOUBLE DEATH,"
ONE LIFE (1957)

There is nothing that war has ever achieved we could not better achieve without it.

—HAVELOCK ELLIS

———•◦•◦•———

Men are so accustomed to maintaining external order by violence that they cannot conceive of life being possible without violence.

—LEO TOLSTOY

———•◦•◦•———

Violence is the last refuge of the incompetent.

—ISAAC ASIMOV, *FOUNDATION* (1951)

My peace is gone,
My heart is heavy.
>   —JOHANN WOLFGANG VON GOETHE, *Faust*,
>   "GRETCHEN'S ROOM" (1909–14)

One is left with the horrible feeling now that war settles *nothing*; that to *win* a war is as disastrous as to lose one!
>   —AGATHA CHRISTIE, *AN AUTOBIOGRAPHY* (1977)

If you wish for peace, understand war.
>   —B. H. LIDDELL HART (MAY 1932), *THOUGHTS ON WAR* (1944)

I was in the midst of it all—saw war where war is worst—not on the battlefields, no—in the hospitals: . . . there I mixed with it: and now I say God damn the wars—all wars: God damn every war: God damn 'em! God damn 'em!

> —WALT WHITMAN (DECEMBER 13, 1888), IN HORACE TRAUBEL, *WALT WHITMAN'S CAMDEN CONVERSATIONS*, ED. WALTER TELLER (1973)

I hate war as only a soldier who has lived it can, only as one who has seen its brutality, its futility, and its *stupidity*.

> —DWIGHT D. EISENHOWER, SPEECH IN OTTAWA, CANADA (JANUARY 10, 1946)

Are you saying that I would have to have fought in the war in order to love peace? . . . It's about as valid as saying that you would have to be black in order to despise racism, that you'd have to be female in order to be terribly offended by sexism. And that's just not so.

—GERALDINE FERRARO, VICE PRESIDENTIAL DEBATE, PHILADELPHIA (OCTOBER 11, 1984)
Commonly cited as "You don't have to have fought in a war to love peace."

The improvement of life was only accomplished to the extent to which it was based on a change of consciousness, that is, to the extent to which the law of violence was replaced in men's consciousness by the law of love.

—LEO TOLSTOY, *THE KINGDOM OF GOD IS WITHIN YOU* (1893), TR. AYLMER MAUDE (1936)

War stirs in men's hearts the mud of their worst instincts. It puts a premium on violence, nourishes hatred, and gives free rein to cupidity. It crushes the weak, exalts the unworthy, and bolsters tyranny.

—CHARLES DE GAULLE

Who would ever have believed that human beings would be stupid enough to blow themselves off the face of the earth? . . . The war started when people accepted the idiotic principle that peace could be maintained by arranging to defend themselves with weapons they couldn't possibly use without committing suicide.

—JOHN PAXTON AND STANLEY KRAMER, LINES SPOKEN BY JULIAN OSBORNE (FRED ASTAIRE) IN *ON THE BEACH* (1959)

Let us not deceive ourself: we must elect world peace or world destruction.

—BERNARD MANNES BARUCH, ADDRESS TO THE UNITED NATIONS ATOMIC ENERGY COMMISSION (JUNE 14, 1946)

War does not determine who is right—only who is left.

—BERTRAND RUSSELL

The only alternative to coexistence is codestruction.

—JAWAHARLAL NEHRU, *LONDON OBSERVER* (AUGUST 29, 1954)

Never have the nations of the world had so much to lose, or so much to gain. Together we shall save our planet, or together we shall perish in its flames.

—JOHN FITZGERALD KENNEDY, ADDRESS TO THE UNITED NATIONS, NEW YORK CITY (SEPTEMBER 25, 1961)

If we do not speak for Earth, who will? If we are not committed to our own survival, who will be?

—CARL SAGAN, *COSMOS* (1980)

We still have a choice today: nonviolent coexistence or violent coannihilation.

—MARTIN LUTHER KING, JR., "BEYOND VIETNAM," ADDRESS AT RIVERSIDE CHURCH, NEW YORK CITY (APRIL 4, 1967)

It is clear that the nations of the world now can only rise and fall together. It is not a question of one nation winning at the expense of another. We must all help one another or all perish together.

—CARL SAGAN, SPEECH ON THE 125TH ANNIVERSARY OF GETTYSBURG, DEDICATING THE PEACE MEMORIAL AT GETTYSBURG NATIONAL CEMETERY PARK (1988)

Violence in the voice is often only the death rattle of reason in the throat.

—JOHN BOYES

One sword keeps another in the sheath.
—GEORGE HERBERT, *JACULA PRUDENTUM* (1651)

Ef you want peace, the thing you've gut tu du
Is jes' to show you're up to fightin', tu.
—JAMES RUSSELL LOWELL, *A FABLE FOR CRITICS* (1848)

Why does man have reason if he can only be influenced by violence?
—LEO TOLSTOY

What we dignify with the name of peace is really only a short truce, in accordance with which the weaker party renounces his claims, whether just or unjust, until such time as he can find an opportunity of asserting them with the sword.

—VAUVENARGUES (MARQUIS OF), REFLECTIONS AND MAXIMS (1746), TR. F. G. STEVENS

No one can have peace longer than his neighbor pleases.

—DUTCH PROVERB

Let him who desires peace prepare for war.

—VEGETIUS (FLAVIUS VEGETIUS RENATUS)

To be prepared for war is one of the most effective means of preserving peace.

—GEORGE WASHINGTON, FIRST ANNUAL ADDRESS TO BOTH HOUSES OF CONGRESS (JANUARY 8, 1790)

The way to prevent war is to bend every energy toward preventing it, not to proceed by the dubious indirection of preparing for it.

—MAX LERNER, "ON PEACETIME MILITARY TRAINING," ACTIONS AND PASSIONS (1949)

The contention that a standing army and navy is the best security of peace is about as logical as the claim that the most peaceful citizen is he who goes about heavily armed.

—EMMA GOLDMAN, *ANARCHISM AND OTHER ESSAYS* (1917)

No one is so foolish as to prefer to peace war, in which, instead of sons burying their fathers, fathers bury their sons.

—CROESUS, REMARK TO KING CYRUS IN HERODOTUS, *THE PERSIAN WARS*, TR. GEORGE RAWLINSON

And blood in torrents pour
In vain—always in vain,
For war breeds war again.
—JOHN DAVIDSON, "WAR SONG" (1899)

And blood in torrents pour

Every war carries within it the war which will answer it. Every war is answered by a new war, until everything, everything is smashed.
—KÄTHE KOLLWITZ (1944), IN HANS KOLLWITZ, ED.,
THE DIARIES AND LETTERS OF KÄTHE KOLLWITZ (1955)

Warmaking doesn't stop warmaking. If it did, our problems would have stopped millennia ago.

—COLMAN MCCARTHY, FROM *WASHINGTON POST* COLUMN "PROWAR MEANS ANTILIFE" (MARCH 3, 1991)

The thesis of the indivisibility of peace. . . . It has now become clear to the whole world that each war is the creation of a preceding war and the generator of new present or future wars.

—MAXIM MAXIMOVICH LITVINOV, SPEECH TO THE LEAGUE OF NATIONS (SEPTEMBER 5, 1935)

And so, to the end of history, murder shall breed murder, always in the name of right and honor and peace, until the gods are tired of blood and create a race that can understand.

—GEORGE BERNARD SHAW, *CAESAR AND CLEOPATRA* (1899)

Everything you do in war is crime in peace.

—HELEN MCCLOY, *A CHANGE OF HEART* (1973)

To my mind, to kill in war is not a whit better than to commit ordinary murder.

—ALBERT EINSTEIN, IN *KAIZO* (AUTUMN 1952)

The State practices "violence," the individual must not do so. The state's behavior is violence, and it calls its violence "law"; that of the individual, "crime."

—MAX STIRNER, *THE EGO AND HIS OWN* (1845), TR. STEVEN T. BYINGTON (1907)

⋅——⋅●⋅——⋅

I have little faith in the theory that organized killing is the best prelude to peace.

—ELLEN GLASGOW, *VEIN OF IRON* (1935)

⋅——⋅●⋅——⋅

"Terrorism" is what we call the violence of the weak, and we condemn it; "war" is what we call the violence of the strong, and we glorify it.

—SYDNEY J. HARRIS, *CLEARING THE GROUND* (1986)

Everything in war is barbaric. . . . But the worst barbarity of war is that it forces men collectively to commit acts against which individually they would revolt with their whole being.

—ELLEN KEY, *WAR, PEACE, AND THE FUTURE* (1916)

———

There's no honorable way to kill, no gentle way to destroy. There is nothing good in war. Except its ending.

—ABRAHAM LINCOLN

My pacifism is not based on any intellectual theory but on a deep antipathy to every form of cruelty and hatred.

—ALBERT EINSTEIN (1914)

———•◆•———

We cannot have peace among men whose hearts delight in killing any living creature. By every act that glorifies or even tolerates such moronic delight in killing we set back the progress of humanity.

—RACHEL CARSON

Fair peace is becoming to men; fierce anger belongs to beasts.

—OVID, *THE ART OF LOVE* (c. A.D. 8)

Whoever fights monsters should see to it that in the process he does not become a monster. And when you look into an abyss, the abyss also looks into you.

—FRIEDRICH WILHELM NIETZSCHE, *BEYOND GOOD AND EVIL* (1886)

The most terrifying monster lurking in the darkness of Hiroshima is precisely the possibility that man might become no longer human.

—KENZABURO OE, *HIROSHIMA NOTES* (1965)

The bomb that fell on Hiroshima fell on America, too.

—HERMANN HAGEDORN, *THE BOMB THAT FELL ON AMERICA* (1946)

You may either win your peace or buy it; win it, by resistance to evil; buy it, by compromise with evil.

—JOHN RUSKIN, *THE TWO PATHS*, LECTURE 5 (1859)

In violence we forget who we are.

—MARY MCCARTHY, *ON THE CONTRARY: ARTICLES OF BELIEF, 1946–1961* (1961)

The finger pulls the trigger, but the trigger may also be pulling the finger.

—DR. LEONARD BERKOWITZ, "IMPULSE, AGGRESSION AND THE GUN," *PSYCHOLOGY TODAY* (SEPTEMBER 1968)

In such a world of conflict, a world of victims and executioners, it is the job of thinking people not to be on the side of the executioners.

—ALBERT CAMUS

It takes twenty years or more of peace to make a man; it takes only twenty seconds of war to destroy him.

—BAUDOUIN I, ADDRESS TO JOINT SESSION OF U.S. CONGRESS (MAY 12, 1959)

That they may have a little peace, even the best dogs are compelled to snarl occasionally.

—WILLIAM FEATHER

It is the ignorant and childish part of mankind that is the fighting part. Idle and vacant minds want excitement, as all boys kill cats.

—RALPH WALDO EMERSON, "WAR," SPEECH TO THE AMERICAN PEACE SOCIETY, BOSTON (1838)

It is easier to lead men to combat and to stir up their passions than to temper them and urge them to the patient labors of peace.

—ANDRÉ GIDE, *JOURNALS*, TR. JUSTIN O'BRIEN (SEPTEMBER 13, 1938)

War will never cease until babies begin to come into the world with larger cerebrums and smaller adrenal glands.

—H. L. MENCKEN, *MINORITY REPORT: H. L. MENCKEN'S NOTEBOOKS* (1956)

A man may build himself a throne of bayonets, but he cannot sit on it.

—WILLIAM RALPH INGE, FROM *WIT AND WISDOM OF DEAN INGE* (1977)

If peace . . . only had the music and pageantry of war, there'd be no wars.

—SOPHIE KERR, *THE MAN WHO KNEW THE DATE* (1951)

—◆◆◆—

War comes at the end of the twentieth century as absolute failure of imagination, scientific and political. That a war can be represented as helping a people to "feel good" about themselves, their country, is a measure of that failure.

—ADRIENNE RICH (JANUARY 1991), *WHAT IS FOUND THERE: NOTEBOOKS ON POETRY AND POLITICS* (1993)

War is death's feast.

—ENGLISH PROVERB

Where peace
And rest can never dwell, hope never comes
That comes to all.

—JOHN MILTON, *PARADISE LOST* (1667)

What they could do with round here is a good war. What else can you expect with peace running wild all over the place? You know what the trouble with peace is? No organization.

—BERTOLT BRECHT, *MOTHER COURAGE AND HER CHILDREN* (1941)

The only thing that's been a worse flop than the organization of nonviolence has been the organization of violence.

—JOAN BAEZ, "WHAT WOULD YOU DO IF?" *DAYBREAK* (1968)

In safety, do not forget danger; in peace, do not forget disorder.

—CHINESE PROVERB

Peace is made by the biggest battalions!

—GEORGES CLEMENCEAU, IN GEORGE SYLVESTER VIERECK, *GLIMPSES OF THE GREAT* (1930)

Wherefore do you so ill translate yourself
Out of the speech of peace that bears such grace,
Into the harsh and boisterous tongue of war?

—WILLIAM SHAKESPEARE, LINES SPOKEN BY WESTMORELAND IN *HENRY IV* (1591)

The legitimate object of war is a more perfect peace.

—WILLIAM TECUMSEH SHERMAN, SPEECH IN ST. LOUIS
(JULY 20, 1865)

Before a war, military science seems a real science,
like astronomy. After a war it seems more like as-
trology.

—REBECCA WEST

We make war that we may live in peace.

—ARISTOTLE, *NICOMACHEAN ETHICS*

If it's natural to kill, how come men have to go into training to learn how?

—JOAN BAEZ, "WHAT WOULD YOU DO IF?"
DAYBREAK (1968)

Until lions have their historians, tales of the hunt shall always glorify the hunters.

—AFRICAN PROVERB

It is obvious that modern war is not good business from a financial point of view. Although we won both the world wars, we should now be much richer if they had not occurred.

—BERTRAND RUSSELL, NOBEL PRIZE IN LITERATURE ACCEPTANCE SPEECH (DECEMBER 11, 1950)

On the whole our armed services have been doing pretty well in the way of keeping us defended, but I hope our State Department will remember that it is really the department of achieving peace.

—ELEANOR ROOSEVELT, FROM HER "MY DAY" COLUMN, PUBLISHED IN THE *LADIES' HOME JOURNAL* (NOVEMBER 11, 1946)

"Needed: A Department of Peace."

—KARL E. MUNDT, TITLE OF SENATE SPEECH (1945)

We have contingency plans for war, but none for peace.

—THEODORE C. SORENSEN, ON THE *TODAY* SHOW (NOVEMBER 1989)

The time has come for man's intellect, his scientific method, to win over the immoral brutality and irrationality of war and militarism. . . . Now we are forced to eliminate from the world forever this vestige of prehistoric barbarism, this curse to the human race.

—LINUS PAULING

These mechanical and scientific achievements of man had outrun his intellectual and spiritual power. . . . We hope our nation will survive, but in its effort to survive will it transform itself intellectually and spiritually into the image of the thing against which we fought?

—VIRGINIA CROCHERON GILDERSLEEVE, *MANY A GOOD CRUSADE* (1954)

The more bombers, the less room for doves of peace.

—NIKITA S. KHRUSHCHEV, MOSCOW RADIO ADDRESS (MARCH 14, 1958)

Technology has allowed the world of men in our society to separate itself from the sight and the sounds of killing; from the horror of it, but not from the killing. It must be easy to kill from a roomful of fluorescent lights and wash-and-wear shirts.

—CARYL RIVERS, "MEN AND WOMEN," IN *GLAMOUR* (1973)

The people who are doing the work and the fighting and the dying, and those who are doing the talking, are not all the same people.

—KATHERINE ANNE PORTER, "AMERICAN STATEMENT" (1942)

There's no difference between one's killing and making decisions that will send others to kill. It's exactly the same thing, or even worse.

—GOLDA MEIR, INTERVIEW (1974)

All wars are wars among thieves who are too cowardly to fight and who therefore induce the young manhood of the whole world to do the fighting for them.

—EMMA GOLDMAN (1917)

———•◦•◦•———

The most shocking fact about war is that its victims and its instruments are individual human beings, and that these individual beings are condemned by the monstrous conventions of politics to murder or be murdered in quarrels not their own.

—ALDOUS HUXLEY, THE OLIVE TREE (1937)

Can anything be more ridiculous than that a man should have the right to kill me because he lives on the other side of the water, and because his ruler has a quarrel with mine, though I have none with him?

—BLAISE PASCAL, *PENSÉES*, TR. W. F. TROTTER (1670)

If you insist upon fighting to protect me, or "our" country, let it be understood soberly and rationally between us that you are fighting to gratify a sex instinct which I cannot share; to procure benefits which I have not shared and probably will not share.

—VIRGINIA WOOLF, *THREE GUINEAS* (1938)

Everyone is always talking about our defense effort in terms of protecting women and children, but no one ever asks the women and children what they think.

—PATRICIA SCHROEDER, IN ESTHER STINEMAN,
AMERICAN POLITICAL WOMEN (1980)

My aunt once said the world would never find peace until men fell at their women's feet and asked for forgiveness.

—JACK KEROUAC, *ON THE ROAD* (1957)

Gandhi once declared that it was his wife who unwittingly taught him the effectiveness of nonviolence. Who better than women should know that battles can be won without resorting to physical strength?

—BARBARA DEMING, *REVOLUTION & EQUILIBRIUM* (1971)

Women are not inherently passive or peaceful. We're not inherently anything but human.

—ROBIN MORGAN

A truly pacifist people would quickly disappear from history.

—GUSTAVE LE BON, *APHORISMS OF PRESENT TIMES* (1913), TR. ALICE WIDENER (1979)

You know, if people are not pacifists, it's not their fault. It's because society puts them in that spot. You've got to change it. You don't just change a man—you've got to change his environment as you do it.

—CESAR CHAVEZ

There will be no lasting peace either in the heart of individuals or in social customs until death is outlawed.

—ALBERT CAMUS, "REFLECTIONS ON THE GUILLOTINE,"
RESISTANCE, REBELLION AND DEATH (1961)

Sometime they'll give a war and nobody will come.

—CARL SANDBURG, *THE PEOPLE, YES* (1936)

War is an old, old plant on this earth, and a natural history of it would have to tell us under what soil conditions it grows, where it plays havoc, and how it is eliminated.

—RUTH BENEDICT (1939), IN MARGARET MEAD, *AN ANTHROPOLOGIST AT WORK* (1959)

I believe in compulsory cannibalism. If people were forced to eat what they killed there would be no more war.

—ABBIE HOFFMAN

War . . . seems a mere madness, a collective insanity.

—BERTRAND RUSSELL, *PRINCIPLES OF SOCIAL RECONSTRUCTION* (1916)

It is right noble to fight with wickedness and wrong; the mistake is in supposing that spiritual evil can be overcome by physical means.

—LYDIA MARIA CHILD, *LETTERS FROM NEW YORK*, VOL. I (1843)

I won't undertake war until I have tried all the arts and means of peace.

—FRANÇOIS RABELAIS, line spoken by GRANDGOUSIER
IN *GARGANTUA*, PLEIADE EDITION (1995)

<hr>

As long as war is regarded as wicked, it will always have its fascination. When it is looked upon as vulgar, it will cease to be popular.

—OSCAR WILDE, "THE CRITIC AS ARTIST,"
INTENTIONS (1891)

War is the unfolding of miscalculations.

—BARBARA W. TUCHMAN, *THE GUNS OF AUGUST* (1962)

If the Nazis have really been guilty of the unspeakable crimes circumstantially imputed to them, then—let us make no mistake—pacifism is faced with a situation with which it cannot cope.

—JOHN MIDDLETON MURRY, *PEACE NEWS* (SEPTEMBER 22, 1944)

Pacifism is simply undisguised cowardice.

—ADOLF HITLER, SPEECH IN NUREMBERG, GERMANY
(AUGUST 21, 1926)

If we could raise one generation with unconditional love, there would be no Hitlers. . . . Mankind's greatest gift, also its greatest curse, is that we have free choice. We can make our choices built from love or from fear.

—ELISABETH KÜBLER-ROSS

A peace is of the nature of a conquest,
For then both parties nobly are subdued,
And neither party loser.

> —WILLIAM SHAKESPEARE, SPOKEN BY ARCHBISHOP OF
> YORK IN *HENRY IV* (1591)

The people who burned witches at the stake never for one moment thought of their act as violence; rather they thought of it as an act of divinely mandated righteousness. The same can be said of most of the violence we humans have ever committed.

> —GIL BAILIE

How can one not speak about war, poverty, and inequality when people who suffer from these afflictions don't have a voice to speak?

—Isabel Allende

It is the people who have no say in making wars who suffer most from the consequences of them.

—Philippa Carr, *The Gossamer Cord* (1992)

Peace, in the sense of the absence of war, is of little value to someone who is dying of hunger or cold. . . . Peace can only last where human rights are respected, where the people are fed, and where individuals and nations are free.

—DALAI LAMA XIV (TENZIN GYATSO), NOBEL PEACE PRIZE ACCEPTANCE SPEECH (DECEMBER 11, 1989)

Peace begins when the hungry are fed.

—ANONYMOUS

Every gun that is made, every warship launched, every rocket fired signifies, in the final sense, a theft from those who hunger and are not fed, those who are cold and are not clothed.

—DWIGHT D. EISENHOWER, "THE CHANCE FOR PEACE," SPEECH BEFORE THE AMERICAN SOCIETY OF NEWSPAPER EDITORS, WASHINGTON, D.C. (APRIL 16, 1953)

When the rich wage war it is the poor who die.

—JEAN-PAUL SARTRE, *THE DEVIL AND THE GOOD LORD* (1951)

A pacifism which can see the cruelties only of occasional military warfare and is blind to the continuous cruelties of our social system is worthless.

—MOHANDAS K. GANDHI, IN *YOUNG INDIA*
(NOVEMBER 18, 1926)

———————

Peace will never be entirely secure until men everywhere have learned to conquer poverty without sacrificing liberty or security.

—NORMAN THOMAS

Wars are bred by poverty and oppression. Continued peace is possible only in a relatively free and prosperous world.

—GEORGE C. MARSHALL (1956)

There is no trust more sacred than the one the world holds with children. There is no duty more important than ensuring that their rights are respected, that their welfare is protected, that their lives are free from fear and want and that they grow up in peace.

—KOFI ANNAN

Peace we want because there is another war to fight against poverty, disease and ignorance.

—INDIRA GANDHI, RADIO BROADCAST
(JANUARY 26, 1966)

The motto of war is: "Let the strong survive; let the weak die." The motto of peace is: "Let the strong help the weak to survive."

—FRANKLIN DELANO ROOSEVELT, SPEECH BEFORE THE
CONGRESS AND SUPREME COURT OF BRAZIL, RIO DE
JANEIRO (NOVEMBER 27, 1936)

While you are proclaiming peace with your lips, be careful to have it even more fully in your heart.

—St. Francis of Assisi

Make love, not war.

—American slogan, 1960s

If this phrase of the "balance of power" is to be always an argument for war, the pretext for war will never be wanting, and peace can never be secure.

—John Bright, speech to House of Commons (March 31, 1854)

Put up again thy sword into his place: for all they that take the sword shall perish with the sword.

—*BIBLE*, MATTHEW 26:52

The history of mankind is crowded with evidences proving . . . that it is only the meek who shall inherit the earth, for the violent, who resort to the sword, are destined to perish with the sword.

—WILLIAM LLOYD GARRISON, DECLARATION OF SENTIMENTS (ADOPTED BY THE PEACE CONVENTION), BOSTON (SEPTEMBER 18–20, 1838)

Freedom achieved by the sword is uniformly lost again, but . . . it is lasting when gained by peaceful agitation.

—HERBERT SPENCER, *SOCIAL STATICS* (1851)

The ballot is stronger than the bullet.

—ABRAHAM LINCOLN, SPEECH IN BLOOMINGTON, ILLINOIS (MAY 19, 1856)

The self-styled intellectual who is impotent with pen and ink hungers to write history with sword and blood.

—ERIC HOFFER, *THE PASSIONATE STATE OF MIND* (1955)

Beneath the rule of men entirely great,
The pen is mightier than the sword.

—EDWARD GEORGE BULWER-LYTTON, *RICHELIEU* (1839)

I really do inhabit a system in which words are capable of shaking the entire structure of government, where words can prove mightier than ten military divisions.

—VÁCLAV HAVEL, SPEECH ACCEPTING A PEACE PRIZE IN GERMANY (OCTOBER 1989)

Because of the realities of human nature, perfect peace is achieved in two places only: in the grave and at the typewriter.

—RICHARD M. NIXON, *REAL PEACE* (1984)

My argument is that War makes rattling good history; but Peace is poor reading.

—THOMAS HARDY, "SPIRIT SINISTER," *THE DYNASTS* (1904–1908)

The grim fact is that we prepare for war like precocious giants and for peace like retarded pygmies.

—LESTER PEARSON, NEWS SUMMARIES (MARCH 15, 1955)

We have grasped the mystery of the atom and rejected the Sermon on the Mount. . . . The world has achieved brilliance without wisdom, power without conscience. Ours is a world of nuclear giants and ethical infants.

—GENERAL OMAR BRADLEY, ADDRESS ON ARMISTICE DAY (NOVEMBER 11, 1948)

To my mind, the nuclear bomb is the most useless weapon ever invented. It can be employed to no rational purpose. It is not even an effective defense against itself.

—GEORGE F. KENNAN (MAY 24, 1981)

The last major childhood disease remains and it's the worst of them all: nuclear war.

—BEVERLY SILLS

It did not take atomic weapons to make man want peace, a peace that would last. But the atomic bomb was the turn of the screw. It has made the prospect of future war unendurable.

—J. ROBERT OPPENHEIMER, *THE ATOMIC BOMB AND COLLEGE EDUCATION* (1946)

If only I had known, I would have become a watch-maker.

—ALBERT EINSTEIN, IN THE *NEW STATESMAN* (April 16, 1955), ON HIS PART IN DEVELOPING THE ATOMIC BOMB

———◆◈◆———

Human history becomes more and more a race be-tween education and catastrophe.

—H. G. WELLS, *THE OUTLINE OF HISTORY* (1920)

Everyone speaks of peace; no one knows what peace is. We know at best a poisoned peace. No one has lived on an earth without weapons, without war and the threat of war on a large and small scale.

—CHRISTINA THÜRMER-ROHR, *VAGABONDING* (1991)

The true and solid peace of nations consists not in equality of arms but in mutual trust alone.

—POPE JOHN XXIII, *PACEM IN TERRIS* (April 11, 1963)

Bullets cannot be recalled. They cannot be unin-vented. But they can be taken out of the gun.
—MARTIN AMIS, *EINSTEIN'S MONSTERS* (1987)

This idea of weapons of mass extermination is ut-terly horrible and is something which no one with one spark of humanity can tolerate. I will not pre-tend to obey a government which is organizing a mass massacre of mankind.
—BERTRAND RUSSELL, SPEECH IN BIRMINGHAM, ENGLAND (APRIL 15, 1961), PROMOTING CIVIL DISOBEDIENCE TO SUPPORT NUCLEAR DISARMAMENT

The pens which write against disarmament are made with the same steel from which guns are made.

—ARISTIDE BRIAND

When nations are able to inflict tens of millions of casualties in a matter of hours, peace has become a moral imperative.

—HENRY A. KISSINGER, *WHITE HOUSE YEARS* (1979)

A liberation movement that is nonviolent sets the oppressor free as well as the oppressed.

—BARBARA DEMING, IN JEANNE LARSON AND MADGE MICHEELS-CYRUS, COMPS., *SEEDS OF PEACE* (1986)

Nonviolence, pacifism, that's the greatest thing that I think the human species has to aspire to, because otherwise it's not going to be around.

—MARTIN SCORSESE, TELEVISION INTERVIEW ON *CHARLIE ROSE* (JANUARY 16, 1998)

The belief that we some day shall be able to prevent war is to me one with the belief in the possibility of making humanity really human.

—ELLEN KEY, *WAR, PEACE, AND THE FUTURE* (1916)

The great question is, can war be outlawed from the world? If so, it would mark the greatest advance in civilization since the Sermon on the Mount.

—DOUGLAS MACARTHUR, SPEECH AT AN AMERICAN
LEGION DINNER, AMBASSADOR HOTEL, LOS ANGELES
(JANUARY 26, 1955)

If man does find the solution for world peace it will be the most revolutionary reversal of his record we have ever known.

—GEORGE C. MARSHALL, BIENNIAL REPORT OF
THE CHIEF OF STAFF, UNITED STATES ARMY
(SEPTEMBER 1, 1945)

———◆———

The pacifist's task today is to find a method of helping and healing which provides a revolutionary constructive substitute for war.

—VERA BRITTAIN, *THE REBEL PASSION* (1964)

Non-violence is not inaction. It is not discussion. It is not for the timid or weak ... Non-violence is hard work. It is the willingness to sacrifice. It is the patience to win.

—CESAR CHAVEZ

Aye, fight! But not your neighbor. Fight rather all the things that cause you and your neighbor to fight.

—MIKHAIL NAIM

We challenge the culture of violence when we ourselves act in the certainty that violence is no longer
acceptable, that it's tired and outdated no matter
how many cling to it in the stubborn belief that it
still works and that it's still valid.

—GERARD VANDERHAAR

What we need is Star Peace and not Star Wars.

—MIKHAIL S. GORBACHEV, SPEECH TO INDIAN
PARLIAMENT, NEW DELHI (NOVEMBER 28, 1986)

If a protracted politics of nonviolent radical change is beyond the bounds of rational hope, let no one delude oneself that humans are long for this world.

—ROBERT C. TUCKER, "PERSONALITY AND POLITICAL LEADERSHIP," *POLITICAL SCIENCE QUARTERLY* (Fall 1977)

There is no time left for anything but to make peace work a dimension of our every waking activity.

—ELISE BOULDING

You have to take chances for peace, just as you must take chances in war. . . . The ability to get to the verge without getting into the war is the necessary art. If you try to run away from it, if you are scared to go to the brink, you are lost.

—JOHN FOSTER DULLES, IN *LIFE* (JANUARY 16, 1956)

To map out a course of action and follow it to an end requires some of the same courage that a soldier needs. Peace has its victories, but it takes brave men and women to win them.

—RALPH WALDO EMERSON

Nonviolent revolution does not seek the liberation simply of a class or race or nation. It seeks the liberation of mankind. It is our experience that violence shifts the burden of suffering and injustice from one group to another. . . . It destroys one authoritarian structure but creates another.

—COUNCIL OF THE WAR RESISTERS' INTERNATIONAL, "ON WARS OF LIBERATION" (AUGUST 17, 1968)

Nonviolence doesn't always work—but violence never does.

—MADGE MICHAELS-CYRUS

But let us not forget that violence does not live alone and is not capable of living alone: it is necessarily interwoven with falsehood. Between them lies the most intimate, the deepest of natural bonds. Violence finds its only refuge in falsehood, falsehood its only support in violence.

—ALEXANDER SOLZHENITSYN, ACCEPTING THE NOBEL PRIZE IN LITERATURE (1970)

The first casualty, when war comes, is truth.

—HIRAM JOHNSON, SENATE SPEECH (1918)

Violence is a lie, for it goes against the truth of our faith, the truth of our humanity. . . . Violence is a crime against humanity, for it destroys the very fabric of society. On my knees I beg you to turn away from the paths of violence.

—POPE JOHN PAUL II, SPEECH IN DROGHEDA, IRELAND (SEPTEMBER 29, 1979)

Morality is contraband in war.

—MOHANDAS K. GANDHI, *NON-VIOLENCE IN PEACE AND WAR*, VOL. 1 (1942)

What we now need to discover in the social realm is the moral equivalent of war: something heroic that will speak to men as universally as war does, and yet will be as compatible with their spiritual selves as war has proven itself to be incompatible.

—WILLIAM JAMES, *THE VARIETIES OF RELIGIOUS EXPERIENCE: A STUDY IN HUMAN NATURE* (1902)

The only thing for a pacifist to do is to find a *substitute* for war: mountains and seafaring are the only ones I know. But it must be something sufficiently serious not to be a game and sufficiently dangerous to exercise those virtues which otherwise get no chance.

—FREYA STARK, *THE COAST OF INCENSE* (1953)

But don't you see . . . what has for centuries raised man above the beast is not the cudgel but an inward music: the irresistible power of unarmed truth, the powerful attraction of its example.

—BORIS PASTERNAK, *DOCTOR ZHIVAGO* (1957), TR. MAX HAYWARD AND MANYA HARARI (1958)

———•⋄•———

It is not enough to say "We must not wage war." It is necessary to love peace and sacrifice for it. . . . We must see that peace represents a sweeter music, a cosmic melody that is far superior to the discords of war.

—MARTIN LUTHER KING, JR., NOBEL PEACE PRIZE ACCEPTANCE SPEECH, OSLO (DECEMBER 11, 1964)

The world will never have lasting peace so long as men reserve for war the finest human qualities. Peace, no less than war, requires idealism and self-sacrifice and a righteous and dynamic faith.

—JOHN FOSTER DULLES (MARCH 9, 1955)

———

[He] alone is truly nonviolent who remains nonviolent even though he has the ability to strike.

—MOHANDAS K. GANDHI, IN *YOUNG INDIA*
(MAY 7, 1925)

Better give your path to a dog than be bitten by him in contesting for the right. Even killing the dog would not cure the bite.

—ABRAHAM LINCOLN, LETTER (OCTOBER 26, 1863)

Hence to fight and conquer in all your battles is not supreme excellence; supreme excellence consists in breaking the enemy's resistance without fighting.

—SUN TZU, THE ART OF WAR (c. 490 B.C.)

The point of nonviolence is to build a floor, a strong new floor, beneath which we can no longer sink. A platform which stands a few feet above napalm, torture, exploitation, poison gas, A and H bombs, the works. Give man a decent place to stand.

—JOAN BAEZ, "WHAT WOULD YOU DO IF?"
DAYBREAK (1968)

Pacifism simply is not a matter of calm looking on; it is work, hard work.

—KÄTHE KOLLWITZ (1944), IN HANS KOLLWITZ, ED.,
THE DIARIES AND LETTERS OF KÄTHE KOLLWITZ (1955)

The more you sweat in peace, the less you bleed in war.

—HYMAN G. RICKOVER, RETIREMENT SPEECH FROM THE U.S. NAVY (1983)

We have thought of peace as the passive and war as the active way of living. The opposite is true. War is not the most strenuous life. It is a kind of rest-cure compared to the task of reconciling our differences.

—M. P. FOLLETT, *THE NEW STATE* (1918)

Being a pacifist between wars is as easy as being a vegetarian between meals.

—AMMON HENNACY

———◆•◆◆———

It isn't enough to talk about peace; one must believe in it. And it isn't enough to believe in it; one must work at it.

—ELEANOR ROOSEVELT, VOICE OF AMERICA RADIO BROADCAST (NOVEMBER 11, 1951)

I am not only a pacifist but a militant pacifist. I am willing to fight for peace. Nothing will end war unless the people themselves refuse to go to war.

—ALBERT EINSTEIN, INTERVIEW WITH G. S. VIERECK (JANUARY 1931)

A pacifist is as surely a traitor to his country and to humanity as is the most brutal wrongdoer.

—THEODORE ROOSEVELT, SPEECH IN PITTSBURGH, PENNSYLVANIA (JULY 27, 1917)

Peace is a militant thing . . . any peace movement must have behind it a higher passion than the desire for war. No one can be a pacifist without being ready to fight for peace and die for peace.

—MARY HEATON VORSE, *A FOOTNOTE TO FOLLY* (1935)

Peace is not a passive but an active condition, not a negation but an affirmation. It is a gesture as strong as war.

—MARY ROBERTS RINEHART (1918), IN JULIA EDWARDS, *WOMEN OF THE WORLD* (1988)

Peace demands the most heroic labor and the most difficult sacrifice. It demands greater heroism than war. It demands greater fidelity to the truth and a much more perfect purity of conscience.
—THOMAS MERTON

Peace hath higher tests of manhood
Than battle ever knew.
—JOHN GREENLEAF WHITTIER, "THE HERO" (1853)

We have war because we are not sufficiently heroic for a life which does not need war.

> —BARTOLOMEO VANZETTI, IN FREDERIC WERTHAM, *A SIGN FOR CAIN: AN EXPLORATION OF HUMAN VIOLENCE* (1966)

I'm not a pacifist. I'm not that brave.

> —PHIL DONAHUE, TELEVISION INTERVIEW (MAY 31, 1988)

I think that people want peace so much that one of these days governments had better get out of the way and let them have it.

> —DWIGHT D. EISENHOWER, TELEVISION BROADCAST (AUGUST 31, 1959)

The thing I would like to do most is to find somehow to bring peace to the world. It has eluded me.

—LYNDON BAINES JOHNSON, IN THE *DALLAS MORNING NEWS* (JANUARY 14, 1969)

I would rather have peace in the world than be President.

—HARRY S. TRUMAN, CHRISTMAS MESSAGE, INDEPENDENCE, MISSOURI (DECEMBER 24, 1948)

Those who can win a war well can rarely make a good peace, and those who could make a good peace would never have won the war.

—WINSTON CHURCHILL, *MY EARLY LIFE* (1930)

Peace hath her victories
No less renown'd than war.

>—JOHN MILTON, "SONNET 16" (MAY 1652)

The real and lasting victories are those of peace, and not of war.

>—RALPH WALDO EMERSON, "WORSHIP," *THE CONDUCT OF LIFE* (1860)

War: first, one hopes to win; then one expects the enemy to lose; then, one is satisfied that he too is suffering; in the end, one is surprised that everyone has lost.

—KARL KRAUS, *DIE FACKEL*, NO. 462/71 (VIENNA, OCTOBER 9, 1917)

It is useless for the sheep to pass resolutions in favour of vegetarianism, while the wolf remains of a different opinion.

—WILLIAM RALPH INGE, "PATRIOTISM," *OUTSPOKEN ESSAYS* (1915)

Victory would mean peace forced upon the losers, a victor's terms imposed upon the vanquished. It would be accepted in humiliation, under duress, at an intolerable sacrifice, and would leave a sting, a resentment, a bitter memory upon which the terms of peace would rest, not permanently, but only as upon quicksand.

—WOODROW WILSON, ADDRESS TO THE U.S. SENATE
(JANUARY 22, 1917)

Peace is much more precious than a piece of land.

—ANWAR AL-SADAT, SPEECH IN CAIRO
(MARCH 8, 1978)

Peace is not a matter of prizes or trophies. It is not the product of a victory or command. It has no finishing line, no final deadline, no fixed definition of achievement.

—OSCAR ARIAS SÁNCHEZ, NOBEL PEACE
PRIZE ACCEPTANCE SPEECH, STOCKHOLM
(DECEMBER 10, 1987)

Peace is a journey of a thousand miles and it must be taken one step at a time.

—LYNDON BAINES JOHNSON, ADDRESS TO THE
GENERAL ASSEMBLY (DECEMBER 17, 1963)

The pursuit of peace resembles the building of a great cathedral. It is the work of a generation. In concept it requires a master-architect; in execution, the labors of many.

—HUBERT H. HUMPHREY, SPEECH IN NEW YORK CITY
(FEBRUARY 17, 1965)

Peace is not only better than war, but infinitely more arduous.

—GEORGE BERNARD SHAW, *HEARTBREAK HOUSE*, (1920)

It is better we disintegrate in peace and not in pieces.

—BENJAMIN NNAMDI AZIKIWE, IN *NEWSWEEK*
(AUGUST 8, 1966)

What is the use of a house if you haven't got a tolerable planet to put it on?

—HENRY DAVID THOREAU, LETTER TO HARRISON BLAKE (MAY 20, 1860)

The struggle to maintain peace is immeasurably more difficult than any military operation.

—ANNE O'HARE MCCORMICK, IN JULIA EDWARDS, *WOMEN OF THE WORLD* (1988)

War is pillage versus resistance and if illusions of magnitude could be transmuted into ideals of magnanimity, peace might be realized.

—MARIANNE MOORE, "COMMENT," *DIAL* (APRIL 1929)

I want to re-echo my hope that we may all work together for a great peace as distinguished from a mean peace.

—WOODROW WILSON, SPEECH AT THE PALAZZO IN MILAN, ITALY (JANUARY 5, 1919)

By its existence, the Peace Movement denies that governments know best; it stands for a different order of priorities: the human race comes first.

—MARTHA GELLHORN, "CONCLUSION," *THE FACE OF WAR* (1959)

The god of Victory is said to be one-handed, but Peace gives victory to both sides.

—RALPH WALDO EMERSON, JOURNAL (SEPTEMBER 1867)

It must be a peace without victory. . . . Only a peace between equals can last.

—WOODROW WILSON, ADDRESS TO THE SENATE (JANUARY 22, 1917)

If a victory is told in detail, one can no longer distinguish it from a defeat.

—JEAN-PAUL SARTRE, *THE DEVIL AND THE GOOD LORD* (1951)

It is true that we have won all our wars, but we have paid for them. We don't want victories anymore.

—GOLDA MEIR, IN *LIFE* (OCTOBER 3, 1969)

You can no more win a war than you can win an earthquake.

—JEANNETTE RANKIN, CAMPAIGN SPEECH (1943), IN HANNAH JOSEPHSON, *JEANNETTE RANKIN: FIRST LADY IN CONGRESS* (1974)

Mankind must put an end to war or war will put an end to mankind.

> —JOHN FITZGERALD KENNEDY, ADDRESS TO THE
> UNITED NATIONS (SEPTEMBER 25, 1961)

Nothing fairer than peace is given to man to know;
Better one peace than countless triumphs.

> —SILIUS ITALICUS (c. 26–101), *PUNICA*

WAR IS OVER!
IF YOU WANT IT

—JOHN LENNON AND YOKO ONO, BILLBOARD MESSAGE
(SIGNED "LOVE AND PEACE FROM JOHN & YOKO")
DECEMBER 16, 1969
*Lennon and Oko's subsequent single, "Happy Xmas
(War Is Over)" was released December 1, 1971*

More than an end to war, we want an end to the
beginnings of all wars.

—FRANKLIN DELANO ROOSEVELT, ADDRESS WRITTEN
FOR JEFFERSON DAY BROADCAST (APRIL 13, 1945)
Roosevelt died on April 12.

I dream of giving birth to a child who will ask: "Mother, what was war?"

—EVE MERRIAM, *PEACEMAKING: DAY BY DAY* (1989)

Our goal must be not peace in our time but peace for all time.

—HARRY S. TRUMAN, INFORMAL REMARKS IN GALESBURG, ILLINOIS (MAY 8, 1950)

And he shall judge among the nations, and shall rebuke many people: and they shall beat their swords into plowshares, and their spears into pruning-hooks: nation shall not lift up sword against nation, neither shall they learn war any more.

—*BIBLE*, ISAIAH 2:4

───•◦•───

Don't tell me peace has broken out—I've gone and brought all these supplies!

—BERTOLT BRECHT, SPOKEN BY MOTHER COURAGE IN *MOTHER COURAGE AND HER CHILDREN* (1939), TR. ERIC BENTLEY (1955)

For the second time in our history, a British Prime Minister has returned from Germany bringing peace with honor. I believe it is peace for our time. . . . Go home and get a nice quiet sleep.

—NEVILLE CHAMBERLAIN, ADDRESS FROM 10 DOWNING STREET, LONDON (SEPTEMBER 30, 1938), AFTER RETURNING FROM THE MUNICH CONFERENCE

The problem after a war is with the victor. He thinks he has just proved that war and violence pay. Who will now teach him a lesson?

—A. J. MUSTE, "CRISIS IN THE WORLD AND IN THE PEACE MOVEMENT," *THE ESSAYS OF A. J. MUSTE*, ED. NAT HENTOFF (1967)

I feel very lonely without a war. Do you feel like that?

—WINSTON CHURCHILL, REMARK TO THE DIARIST (JUNE 22, 1945), IN *LORD MORAN, CHURCHILL: TAKEN FROM THE DIARIES OF LORD MORAN* (1966)

I love war and responsibility and excitement. Peace is going to be Hell on me.

—GEORGE S. PATTON, JR., LETTER TO HIS WIFE, BEATRICE (APRIL 12, 1945)

To many men . . . the miasma of peace seems more suffocating than the bracing air of war.

—GEORGE STEINER, BRONOWSKI MEMORIAL LECTURE, "HAS TRUTH A FUTURE?" (1978)

It would be naive to think that peace and justice can be achieved easily. No set of rules or study of history will automatically resolve the problems. . . . However, with faith and perseverance, . . . complex problems in the past have been resolved in our search for justice and peace.

—JIMMY CARTER, *NEGOTIATION: THE ALTERNATIVE TO HOSTILITY* (1984)

It is not possible to create peace in the Middle East by jeopardizing the peace of the world.

> —ANEURIN BEVAN, AT RALLY PROTESTING BRITAIN'S ARMED INTERVENTION IN THE SUEZ DISPUTE (NOVEMBER 4, 1956)

Let there be no more war or bloodshed between Arabs and Israelis. Let there be no more suffering or denial of rights. Let there be no more despair or loss of faith.

> —ANWAR AL-SADAT, ON SIGNING THE EGYPTIAN-ISRAELI PEACE TREATY, WASHINGTON, D.C. (MARCH 26, 1979)

No more wars, no more bloodshed. Peace unto you.
Shalom, salaam, forever.

—MENACHEM BEGIN, ON SIGNING THE EGYPTIAN-
ISRAELI PEACE TREATY, WASHINGTON, D.C.
(MARCH 26, 1979)

We are destined to live together on the same soil in
the same land. We, the soldiers who have returned
from the battle stained with blood . . . we who have
fought against you, the Palestinians—we say to you
today in a loud and clear voice: Enough of blood
and tears! Enough!

—YITZHAK RABIN, ON SIGNING THE PALESTINIAN-
ISRAELI PEACE AGREEMENT, WASHINGTON, D.C.
(SEPTEMBER 13, 1993)

This is peace with dignity. This is peace with commitment. This is our gift to our peoples and the generations to come. . . . It will be real, as we open our hearts and minds to each other.

—IBN TALAL HUSSEIN, KING OF JORDAN, IN THE *NEW YORK TIMES* (OCTOBER 27, 1994), ON THE OCCASION OF THE SECOND PEACE ACCORD BETWEEN ISRAEL AND JORDAN, AT A MEETING WITH ISRAELI PRIME MINISTER YITZHAK RABIN

Would to God these blessed calms would last. But the mingled, mingling threads of life are woven by warp and woof: calms crossed by storms, a storm for every calm.

—HERMAN MELVILLE, *MOBY-DICK* (1851)

In Italy for thirty years under the Borgias they had warfare, terror, murder, bloodshed, but they produced Michelangelo, Leonardo da Vinci, and the Renaissance. In Switzerland, they had brotherly love; they had five hundred years of democracy and peace. And what did that produce? The cuckoo clock.

—ORSON WELLES, SPEECH ADDED TO *THE THIRD MAN* (1949)

The pursuit of peace and progress cannot end in a few years in either victory or defeat. The pursuit of peace and progress, with its trials and errors, its successes and setbacks, can never be relaxed and never abandoned.

—DAG HAMMARSKJÖLD

If peace cannot be maintained with honour, it is no longer peace.

—LORD JOHN RUSSELL, SPEECH IN GREENOCK, SCOTLAND (SEPTEMBER 19, 1853)

Most people think of peace as a state of Nothing Bad Happening, or Nothing Much Happening. Yet if peace is to overtake us and make us the gift of serenity and well-being, it will have to be the state of Something Good Happening.

—E. B. WHITE, "UNITY," *ESSAYS OF E. B. WHITE* (1977)

I do not want the peace which passeth understanding. I want the understanding which bringeth peace.

—HELEN KELLER

When the
Power of Love
Overcomes the
Love of Power
The World Will
Know Peace

—ANONYMOUS (AMERICAN), INSCRIBED ON A SOLDIER'S
CIGARETTE LIGHTER, IN A PHOTOGRAPH ACCOMPANYING
MALCOLM W. BRONE, "VIETNAM MEMORABILIA OF A WAR
BEST FORGOTTEN," *NEW YORK TIMES* (APRIL 24, 1994)
Also attributed to William Gladstone

No more war, war never again! Peace, it is peace
which must guide the destinies of people and of all
mankind.

—POPE PAUL VI, UNITED NATIONS ADDRESS, NEW
YORK CITY (OCTOBER 4, 1965)

nothing we do has the quickness, the sureness,
the deep intelligence living at peace would have.
—DENISE LEVERTOV, "LIFE AT WAR" (1968)

Poetry is an act of peace. Peace goes into the making of a poet as flour goes into the making of bread.
—PABLO NERUDA, *RESIDENCIA EN LA TIERRA (RESIDENCE ON EARTH)* (1947)

The fragrance always remains in the hand that gives the rose.

—HEDA BEJAR, IN *PEACEMAKING: DAY BY DAY*, VOL. 2

If there is light in the soul, there will be beauty in the person. If there is beauty in the person, there will be harmony in the house. If there is harmony in the house, there will be order in the nation. If there is order in the nation, there will be peace in the world.

—CHINESE PROVERB

We can best help you to prevent war not by repeating your words and following your methods but by finding new words and creating new methods.

—VIRGINIA WOOLF, *THREE GUINEAS* (1938)

Better than a thousand hollow words
Is one word that brings peace.

—BUDDHA, *THE DHAMMAPADA*

I can feel the sufferings of millions and yet, if I look up into the heavens, I think that it will all come right, that this cruelty too will end, and that peace and tranquility will return again.

—ANNE FRANK, *DIARY OF A YOUNG GIRL* (1947) ENTRY DATED JULY 15, 1944

Ring out old shapes of foul disease,
Ring out the narrowing lust of gold;
Ring out the thousand wars of old,
Ring in the thousand years of peace.

—ALFRED TENNYSON, "IN MEMORIAM" (1850)

If you want to say that I was a drum major, say that I was a drum major for justice. Say that I was a drum major for peace. I was a drum major for right-eousness.

—MARTIN LUTHER KING, JR., SERMON AT
EBENEZER BAPTIST CHURCH, ATLANTA, GEORGIA
(FEBRUARY 4, 1968)

Let the efforts of us all, prove that he [Martin Luther King, Jr.] was not a mere dreamer when he spoke of the beauty of genuine brotherhood and peace being more precious than diamonds or silver or gold.

Let a new age dawn!

—NELSON MANDELA, NOBEL PEACE PRIZE
ACCEPTANCE SPEECH (DECEMBER, 1993)

Blessed are the peacemakers: for they shall be called the children of God.

—*BIBLE*, MATTHEW 5:9

We shall find peace. We shall hear the angels, we shall see the sky sparkling with diamonds.

—ANTON PAVLOVICH CHEKHOV

Peace, it's wonderful.

—FATHER DIVINE (GEORGE BAKER), MOTTO OF THE
PEACE MISSION MOVEMENT

Peace is always beautiful.

—WALT WHITMAN, "THE SLEEPERS," *LEAVES OF
GRASS* (1855)

Contributors' Biographies

Gerry Adams (Gerard Adams) (1948–) is the president of Sinn Féin, the Northern Ireland political party. Once a suspected terrorist, Adams recently called for an end to the violence in Ireland and has twice been elected to the British Parliament (although he has refused to take his seat).

Jane Addams (1860–1935) was a feminist, pacifist, and social worker who founded Hull House in Chicago. She was president of the Women's International League for Peace and Freedom and shared the 1931 Nobel Peace Prize with Nicholas Murray Butler.

Alfred Adler (1870–1937) was an Austrian psychologist and author, an early associate of Sigmund Freud who broke with Freud to study inferiority complexes and social forces.

Aesop, according to legend, was a Greek slave who lived in the sixth century B.C. and was freed by his master. His fables have undergone numerous translations.

Isabel Allende (1942–) is a Chilean novelist—the niece of Salvador Allende, a former president of Chile—who is best known for her first book, *The House of Spirits*.

Anwar al-Sadat (1918–81) was the president of Egypt from 1970 to 1981. He shared the 1978 Nobel Peace Prize with Israeli prime minister Menachem Begin for their efforts to negotiate peace at Camp David. Sadat was assassinated by Muslim extremists.

Henri Amiel (1821–81) was a Swiss critic whose *Journal intime* was published posthumously.

Martin Amis (1949–) is a British novelist whose books include *The Rachel Papers*, *Money*, and *The Information*.

Marian Anderson (1897–1993) was an American opera singer, the first African-American to join the Metropolitan Opera Company, and the first to sing at the White House.

Kofi Annan (1938–), a Ghanaian diplomat and the current secretary-general of the United Nations, is the first black secretary-general in the organization's history. He was elected to the position in 1997 and was awarded the Nobel Peace Prize in 2001.

Aristotle (384–322 B.C.), the Greek philosopher and scientist, studied under Plato at the Academy in Athens and tutored Alexander the Great before opening his own school.

Matthew Arnold (1822–88) was a prominent English poet and critic and a professor of poetry at Oxford from 1857 to 1867.

Isaac Asimov (1920–1992) was an American scientist and science-fiction writer whose books include *I, Robot* and *The Foundation Trilogy*.

W. H. Auden (Wystan Hugh Auden) (1907–73) was a British-born poet and playwright who won the 1947 Pulitzer Prize in Poetry, for *The Age of Anxiety*.

Marcus Aurelius (121–180) was the emperor of Rome from 169 until his death.

Benjamin Nnamdi Azikiwe (1904–96) became the Republic of Nigeria's first president in 1963 and was deposed in a military coup in 1966.

Joan Baez (1941–) is a singer, songwriter, and political activist; a contemporary of Bob Dylan, she helped popularize folk music in the 1960s.

Gil Bailie, president and founder of the Florilegia Institute, a Christian educational center, is the author of *Violence Unveiled: Humanity at the Crossroads*.

Bernard Mannes Baruch (1870–1965) was chairman of the War Industries Board (1918–1919), helped draft the Versailles Treaty, and served as U.S. representative to the U.N. Atomic Energy Commission in 1946.

Baudouin I (1930–93) was the king of Belgium from 1951 to 1993, succeeding his father, Leopold III, upon Leopold's abdication.

Pierre Bayle (1647–1706) was a French philosopher whose primary work was *Dictionnaire historique et critique*.

Menachem Begin (1913–92) was prime minister of Israel from 1977 to 1983. He shared the 1978 Nobel Peace Prize with Egyptian president Anwar al-Sadat for the peace treaty they signed at Camp David.

Saint Robert Bellarmine (1542–1621) was an Italian theologian, cardinal, and archbishop who published several major works of Catholic doctrine; he was canonized by Pope Pius XI in 1930.

Ruth Fulton Benedict (1887–1948) was an anthropologist whose work disputed notions of racism and ethnocentrism prevalent in the 1930s; she was the author of *Patterns of Culture* (about primitive societies), among other books.

Leonard Berkowitz (1926–) is a social psychologist, specializing in human aggression, who taught at the University of Wisconsin.

Daniel Berrigan (1921–) is an American Catholic priest, poet, and social activist.

Aneurin Bevan (1897–1960), a British Labour politician, was a member of Parliament from 1929 to 1960 and the minister of health from 1945 to 1951.

Ambrose Bierce (1842–unknown) was an American satirist, journalist, and short-story writer; he disappeared in Mexico in 1913.

William Blake (1757–1827) was an English Romantic poet and artist whose most famous works of poetry are *Songs of Innocence* and *Songs of Experience*.

Frank Borman (1928–), a former NASA astronaut, commanded Gemini 7 and Gemini 8, the latter of which was the first mission to orbit the moon. He was inducted into the Astronaut Hall of Fame in 1993.

Elise Boulding (1920–), a Norwegian-born sociologist, is professor emerita at Dartmouth College; she helped to establish the U.S. Peace Institute and the International Peace Research Association.

General Omar Bradley (1893–1981) was a U.S. general in World War II; he later served as chief of staff of the army, the first permanent chairman of the Joint Chief of Staffs, and general of the army.

Bertolt Brecht (1898–1956) was a German Marxist poet and playwright whose experimental theater and philosophy of nihilism forced him into exile in Denmark and the United States.

Aristide Briand (1862–1932) served as the French premier eleven times, beginning in 1909. He shared the Nobel Peace Prize with Gustav Stresemann in 1926.

John Bright (1811–89) was a British member of Parliament and later a cabinet member under William Gladstone.

Vera Brittain (1893–1970) was a British writer and pacifist whose memoir, *Testament of Youth*, described her experiences during World War I.

Charlotte Brontë (1816–55), the eldest of the three Brontë sisters, was most celebrated for her novel *Jane Eyre*.

Buddha (Siddhartha Gautama) (c. 563–c. 480 B.C.), the founder of Buddhism, was a Himalayan prince who gave up his family and his material possessions to seek enlightenment. *Buddha* means "enlightened one" in Sanskrit.

Edward George Bulwer-Lytton (1803–73) was an English baron, novelist, playwright, and member of Parliament. He is perhaps best known today for the opening words to his novel *Paul Clifford*: "It was a dark and stormy night."

Samuel Butler (1835–1902) was an English writer whose most widely recognized work is the autobiographical novel *The Way of All Flesh*.

Albert Camus (1913–60) was a French journalist, essayist, and playwright who was awarded the Nobel Prize in Literature in 1957.

Philippa Carr (1906–93) was one of three pseudonyms for Eleanor Hibbert, an author of romantic suspense novels. Under the name Philippa Carr, she published her St. Bruno series, a family saga.

Rachel Carson (1907–64) was an American marine biologist whose landmark book *Silent Spring* studied the hazards of insecticides.

Jimmy Carter (James Earl Carter, Jr.) (1924–), was the thirty-ninth president of the United States. He facilitated a peace treaty between Egypt and Israel but also failed to negotiate the release of several Americans taken hostage in Iran.

Pablo Casals (1876–1973) was a Spanish cellist, pianist, composer, and conductor who performed at the United Nations, the White House, and Lincoln Center, where he conducted eighty cellists.

Ajahn Chah (Pra Bhodinyana Thera) (1917–92) was a Buddhist monk who established the Wat Pa Pong monastary in Thailand; it now has branches in six countries.

Neville Chamberlain (Arthur Neville Chamberlain) (1869–1940) was prime minister of Great Britain from 1937 to 1940. He signed the Munich Pact in 1938 to avoid war with Hitler, but led Britain into World War II in 1939.

Cesar Chavez (1927–93), an American labor leader who organized Mexican and Mexican-American migrant workers, was president of the United Farm Workers and led a boycott against grape growers in 1968.

Anton Pavlovich Chekhov (1860–1904) was a Russian author, playwright, and physician whose plays include *The Seagull*, Uncle *Vanya*, and *The Three Sisters*.

Lydia Maria Child (1802–80) was an American author and abolitionist who edited the *National Anti-Slavery Standard*, a New York weekly newspaper.

Agatha Christie (Dame Agatha Christie) (1891–1976) was the English author of more than eighty mystery novels. She was awarded an Order of the British Empire in 1971.

Winston Churchill (Sir Winston Leonard Spencer Churchill) (1874–1965) was prime minister of Great Britain from 1940 to 1945 and from 1951 to 1955. He was knighted in 1953 and awarded the Nobel Prize in Literature in 1953.

Cicero (Marcus Tullius Cicero) (106–43 B.C.) was a Roman orator, philosopher, and politician who opposed Julius Caesar and was briefly the governor of Cilicia.

Eldridge Cleaver (1935–98) was a member of the African-American militant Black Panther Party and the author of *Soul on Ice*.

Georges Clemenceau (1841–1929) was the premier of France from 1906 to 1909 and from 1917 to 1920.

Richard Cobden (1804–65), a British politician and advocate of free trade, was elected to Parliament in 1841.

Alexander Cockburn (1941–) is a radical journalist who was raised in Ireland and lives in the United States; he contributes regular columns to the *Los Angeles Times*, *The Nation*, and other publications.

Joseph Conrad (1857–1924) was an English novelist born of Polish parents; his novels and novellas include *Lord Jim*, *Heart of Darkness*, and *The Secret Agent*.

Mason Cooley (1927–), an aphorist, is the author of *City Aphorisms*.

Anna Julia Cooper (1859–1964) was an American educator and feminist. The daughter of a slave and a white slaveholder, she became the fourth African-American woman to earn a Ph.D.

Norman Cousins (1915–90), a former editor for the *Saturday Review of Literature*, is best known for his book *Anatomy of an Illness*, in which he wrote about the healing powers of laughter and positive thinking.

Croesus was the king of Lydia from 560 to 546 B.C.

Oliver Cromwell (1599–1658), a soldier and statesman, ruled the British Commonwealth as lord protector from 1653 to 1658, after helping to overthrow King Charles I in a civil war.

Dalai Lama XIV (Tenzin Gyatso) (1935–) is the current leader of Tibetan Buddhism; he lives in exile in India and received the Nobel Peace Prize in 1989.

John Davidson (1857–1909) was a Scottish poet who wrote ballads, plays, and novels.

Dorothy Day (1897–1980), an American journalist and religious leader, co-founded the Catholic Worker Movement and established several houses for the poor and the homeless.

Moshe Dayan (1915–81) held several prominent Israeli government positions (including chief of staff and minister of defense) before becoming foreign minister in 1977, under Menachem Begin.

Catherine de Hueck Doherty (1896–1985) was a Russian-born nurse, missionary, and writer who founded the Madonna House in Ontario, Canada, and the Harlem Friendship House in New York.

Charles de Gaulle (1890–1970) was a French general in World War I and undersecretary of war in World War II; he was president of France from 1959 to 1969.

David Dellinger, an antiwar organizer and political activist, was a member of the Chicago Eight, the group tried for disrupting the 1968 Democratic National Convention. He is the author of *From Yale to Jail: The Life Story of a Moral Dissenter*.

Barbara Deming (1917–84) was a poet, short-story writer, pacifist, and radical feminist who wrote about women's and lesbian issues in such publications as *The Nation* and *Quest*.

Democritus (c. 460–c. 370 B.C.) was a Greek philosopher and student of Leucippus.

Morarji Ranchhodji Desai (1896–1995), leader of the conservative opposition to Indira Gandhi, was prime minister of India from 1977 to 1979.

Charles Dickens (1812–70) was an English novelist whose novels include *A Christmas Carol*, *David Copperfield*, *Bleak House*, and *Great Expectations*.

Phil Donahue (1935–) is a talk-show host whose *The Phil Donahue Show* aired for thirty years.

John Donne (1572–1631) was an English metaphysical poet whose most famous poems include the sonnet "Death Be Not Proud."

John Foster Dulles (1888–1959) was the secretary of state under Dwight D. Eisenhower; he also served as U.S. delegate to the United Nations and as a U.S. senator from New York.

Albert Einstein (1879–1955) was a German-born physicist famed for his work on the theory of relativity and quantum theory; he won the Nobel Prize in Physics in 1921.

Dwight D. Eisenhower (1890–1969) held several top military positions, including that of five-star army general and Allied military commander, before becoming a two-term U.S. president in 1953.

Havelock Ellis (1859–1939) was an English psychologist and author whose major work was the seven-volume series *Studies in the Psychology of Sex*.

Ralph Waldo Emerson (1803–82) was an American transcendentalist poet and essayist, a former minister who co-founded the magazine *The Dial*. His lectures were collected in his series of *Essays* and other books.

Father Divine (George Baker) (c. 1882–1965) was an African-American religious leader and the founder of the Peace Mission Movement.

Geraldine Ferraro (1935–) served three terms in the U.S. House of Representatives before becoming Walter Mondale's running mate in the 1984 presidential election. She was the first female vice-presidential candidate to be nominated by a major party.

M. P. Follett (Mary Parker Follett) (1868–1933) was a social theorist who wrote about organizations and management.

Anne Frank (1929–45) was a German-born Jewish girl; while hiding in an Amsterdam attic with her family to escape persecution by the

Nazis, she kept a diary that was published after her death in the Bergen-Belsen concentration camp.

Benjamin Franklin (1706–90) was a prominent statesman in the American Revolution, a member of the committee that drafted the Declaration of Independence, the author of *Poor Richard's Almanack*, and the inventor of bifocal glasses.

R. Buckminster Fuller (Richard Buckminster Fuller) (1895–1983) was an American engineer and architect whose books include *Operating Manual for Spaceship Earth*.

Indira Gandhi (1917–84) was prime minister of India from 1977 to 1988 and from 1980 to 1984, when she was assassinated by her security guards. Her father was Jawaharlal Nehru.

Mohandas K. Gandhi (Mohandas Karamchand Gandhi) (1869–1948) was an Indian political and spiritual leader who advocated nonviolent civil disobedience. He was given the title Mahatma (great soul) and played a prominent role in the nationalist party, the Indian National Congress.

William Lloyd Garrison (1805–79) was an abolitionist who served as president of the American Anti-Slavery Society, which he helped found.

Martha Gellhorn (1908–1998) was an American journalist and fiction writer who reported on the Spanish Civil War, World War II, the Vietnam War, and conflicts in the Middle East and Central America.

André Gide (1869–1951) was a French novelist, essayist, and playwright who was awarded the Nobel Prize in Literature in 1947.

Virginia Crocheron Gildersleeve (1877–1965) was a professor and dean at Barnard College in New York, as well as founder and president of the International Federation of University Women.

Ellen Glasgow (1874–1945) was a novelist who wrote frequently on her native Virginia. She won the 1942 Pulitzer Prize for her last published novel, *In This Our Life*.

Johann Wolfgang von Goethe (1749–1832) was a German poet, novelist, and playwright whose most famous work is the dramatic poem *Faust*.

Emma Goldman (1869–1940) emigrated from Lithuania to the United States, where she became a prominent anarchist; she was imprisoned several times (once for advocating birth control) and eventually deported.

Mikhail S. Gorbachev (1931–) was general-secretary of the Communist Party of the Soviet Union from 1985 to 1991. He was awarded the Nobel Peace Prize in 1990.

Germaine Greer (1939–) is an Australian feminist writer who first achieved celebrity with her book *The Female Eunuch*.

Louise Imogen Guiney (1861–1920) was a Catholic poet and essayist.

Dag Hammarskjöld (1905–61) was secretary-general of the United Nations from 1953 to 1961. He was posthumously awarded the Nobel Peace Prize in 1961.

Thomas Hardy (1840–1928) was an English novelist and poet whose books include *The Return of the Native, Tess of the D'Urbervilles,* and *Jude the Obscure.*

Sydney J. Harris (1917–1986) was a syndicated newspaper columnist and the author of several books. His column "Strictly Personal" ran daily for more than forty years.

B. H. Liddell Hart (Basil Henry Liddell Hart) (1895–1970) was military correspondent for the London *Daily Times* and the London *Times* after World War I and later personal adviser to the British war minister Leslie Hore-Belisha. He was knighted in 1966.

Václav Havel (1936–), an essayist and playwright, was president of Czechoslovakia from 1989 to 1992; he was elected president of the Czech Republic in 1993 and reelected in 1998.

Ammon Hennacy (1893–1970) was a Christian anarchist and pacifist who spoke, picketed, and fasted in protest of capital punishment and war.

Patrick Henry (1736–99) was a political activist during the American Revolution. He served twice as governor of Virginia and was instrumental in adding the Bill of Rights to the Constitution.

George Herbert (1593–1633) was an English poet and an ordained Anglican priest.

Herodotus (c. 484–425 B.C.), a Greek historian sometimes referred to as the Father of History, is known primarily for his epic narrative history of the Persian Wars.

Herman Hesse (1877–1962), a German-Swiss novelist, essayist, poet, and critic, won the Nobel Prize in Literature in 1946. His books include *Siddartha* and *Steppenwolf*.

Napoleon Hill (1883–1970) was a reporter, educator, and motivational author who wrote *Think and Grow Rich*.

Etty Hillesum (1914–1943) was a Dutch Jewish woman whose diary, which she kept for two years after Germany invaded the Netherlands, was published as *An Interrupted Life and Letters from Westerbork*. She died in Auschwitz at the age of twenty-nine.

Adolf Hitler (1889–1945), the founder and chairman of the National Socialist German workers, or Nazi, party, was chancellor of Germany from 1933 until his death in 1945.

Eric Hoffer (1902–1983) was an American self-educated social philosopher who wrote nine books, among them *The True Believer: Thoughts on the Nature of Mass Movements*.

Abbie Hoffman (1936–89) co-founded the Youth International Party ("Yippies") and was a member of the Chicago Eight, the group tried for disrupting the 1968 Democratic National Convention. He was the author of the book *Steal This Book*.

Gerard Manley Hopkins (1844–89) was an English poet and Jesuit priest whose poems include "The Wreck of the *Deutschland*."

Hubert H. Humphrey (1911–78) was vice president under Lyndon Johnson from 1965 to 1969. Prior to that, he was a longtime U.S. senator from Minnesota.

ibn Talal Hussein (1935–) has been the king of Jordan since 1953.

Aldous Huxley (1894–1963), an English author, is best known for his novel *Brave New World*, about a utopian society in the twenty-fifth century.

Thomas Henry Huxley (1825–95) was an English biologist and advocate of Darwinism.

William Ralph Inge (1860–1964) was the dean of St. Paul's Cathedral in London from 1911 to 1934. He wrote several books on mysticism.

Silius Italicus (26–101) was a Latin poet, orator, and diplomat whose *Punica*, on the second Punic War, is recognized as the longest of the surviving Roman epics.

William James (1842–1910), an American philosopher, was the brother of the novelist Henry James; he taught at Harvard and published the influential *Principles of Psychology*.

Hiram Johnson (1866–1945) was a U.S. senator from California from 1917 to 1945.

Lyndon Baines Johnson (1908–73) was the thirty-sixth president of the United States, taking office after the death of John F. Kennedy. Johnson's presidency was dominated by the Vietnam War.

Samuel Johnson (1709–84) was a leading English critic and scholar who was immortalized in James Boswell's *The Life of Samuel Johnson, L.L.D.*

Julia Ward Howe (1819–1910), an American suffragist and abolitionist, wrote "The Battle Hymn of the Republic" and was the first woman to be admitted into the American Academy of Arts and Letters.

Juvenal (Decimus Junius Juvenalis) (first to second century A.D.) was a Roman satirical poet.

Helen Keller (1880–1968), blind and deaf since the age of two, was famously taught by Anne Sullivan; Keller graduated from Radcliffe and lectured widely on issues concerning the blind and other social causes.

George F. Kennan (1904–), a diplomat and historian, was a chief adviser to U.S. secretary of state Dean Acheson, U.S. ambassador to the USSR, and U.S. ambassador to Yugoslavia.

John Fitzgerald Kennedy (1917–63) was the thirty-fifth president of the United States. He was assassinated in a motorcade in Dallas in 1963.

Jack Kerouac (1922–69), a leader of the 1960s Beat generation of writers and artists, was the author of *On the Road* and other novels.

Sophie Kerr (1880–1965) was a prolific novelist, short-story writer, and journalist who was managing editor of the *Women's Home Companion* magazine.

Ellen Key (1849–1925) was a Swedish author and critic, an anti-feminist who believed women were best suited to motherhood.

Ken Keyes, Jr., a spiritualist and pacifist, was the author of *Handbook to Higher Consciousness* and *The Hundredth Monkey*, which warned of the dangers of nuclear power. He died in 1995.

Nikita S. Khrushchev (1894–1971) was a close associate of Stalin and the premier of the Soviet Union from 1958 to 1964.

Martin Luther King, Jr. (1929–68) was an African-American minister and civil rights leader who received the Nobel Peace Prize in 1964.

Henry A. Kissinger (1923–) was the U.S. secretary of state under Richard Nixon and Gerald Ford.

Käthe Kollwitz (1867–1945) was a German printmaker, sculptor, and socialist who taught at the Academie Julien and co-founded, with Albert Einstein and Upton Sinclair, the International Workers Aid.

Karl Kraus (1874–1936) was an Austrian essayist and poet.

Elizabeth Kübler-Ross (1926–) is a psychiatrist and the author of *On Death and Dying*, which chronicles the five stages of dealing with death.

D. H. Lawrence (David Herbert Lawrence) (1885–1930) was an English novelist whose works include *Sons and Lovers* and *Women in Love*.

Gustave Le Bon (1841–1931) was a French psychologist and sociologist who wrote frequently about racial superiority.

Fran Lebowitz is a New York writer known for her irreverent wit; hired by Andy Warhol to write a column for *Interview* in the 1970s, she has published two books of essays, *Metropolitan Life* and *Social Studies*.

Louis Lecoin (1888–1971) was a French anarchist, pacifist, libertarian, and author.

Barbara Lee is a U.S. congresswoman from California.

John Lennon (1940–80), an English songwriter and musician, was a founding member of the rock group the Beatles and a successful solo artist after the band's breakup.

Max Lerner (1902–92) was an American author, educator, and syndicated columnist.

Denise Levertov (1923–97) was a poet, essayist, translator, and political activist who lived in England and the United States.

Georg Christoph Lichtenberg (1742–99) was a German physicist and satirist.

Abraham Lincoln (1809–65) was the sixteenth president of the United States, leading the country through the Civil War before being shot and killed at Ford's Theater.

Walter Lippman (1889–1974) was an editor, author, and syndicated columnist who co-founded *The New Republic* and, as a member of Woodrow Wilson's administration, helped to draft Wilson's Fourteen Points.

Maxim Maximovich Litvinov (1876–1951) was Soviet commissar for foreign affairs in the 1930s and later ambassador to the United States.

Livy (59 B.C.–A.D. 17) was a Roman historian whose major work was his *History of Rome,* which covered the period from 753 B.C. to 9 B.C.

Henry Wadsworth Longfellow (1807–82) was an American narrative poet who wrote *The Song of Hiawatha* and "Paul Revere's Ride," a poem from *Tales of a Wayside Inn.*

James Russell Lowell (1819–91), a poet and critic, was the first editor of the *Atlantic Monthly* and the *North American Review.*

Max Lucado is a minister, radio host, and the author of several best-selling adult and children's books about Christianity.

Martin Luther (1483–1546) was a German priest and the leader of the Protestant Reformation.

Robert Lynd (1892–1970) was a sociology professor at Columbia University and a labor and civil rights activist.

Douglas MacArthur (1880–1964) was a five-star U.S. army general who commanded forces in World War I, World War II, and the Korean War.

Colman McCarthy, a former newspaper columnist for the *Washington Post*, founded the Center for Teaching Peace in 1982 and is the author of several books, among them *All of One Peace: Essays on Nonviolence*.

Mary McCarthy (1912–89) was an American novelist, essayist, critic, and activist whose books include *The Group* and the memoir *Memories of a Catholic Girlhood*.

Helen McCloy (1904–94) was an American mystery writer whose novels, including *Through a Glass, Darkly*, often featured the psychiatrist detective Basil Willing. She was the first woman president of Mystery Writers of America.

Anne O'Hare McCormick (1880–1954) was a foreign-affairs correspondent and columnist for the *New York Times*; she won a Pulitzer Prize in Journalism in 1937.

Nelson Mandela (1918–), a South African political leader, spent more than two decades in prison before being pardoned by President F. W. de Clerk in 1990. After the two men were awarded the Nobel Peace Prize in 1993, Mandela was elected president in the nation's first multiracial elections, serving from 1994 to 1998.

Christopher Marlowe (1564–93) was an English poet and playwright whose work influenced Shakespeare. Among his many works are the play *The Jew of Malta* and the poem *Hero and Leander.*

George C. Marshall (1880–1959) was U.S. Army chief of staff and then five-star general of the army in World War II; he served as secretary of state under President Truman and was awarded the Nobel Peace Prize in 1953 for his Marshall Plan.

Margaret Mead (1901–78) was an anthropologist, author, curator of ethnology at the American Museum of Natural History, and a professor at Columbia University.

Golda Meir (1898–1978) was the Israeli minister to Moscow, minister of labor, foreign minister, and finally prime minister (from 1969 to 1974).

Herman Melville (1819–91) was an American novelist and poet whose most famous novel, *Moby-Dick,* went unheralded until thirty years after his death.

H. L. Mencken (Henry Louis Mencken) (1880–1956) was an author, editor, and critic who edited the Baltimore *Evening Herald* and was on the staff of the Baltimore *Sun* from 1906 until his death.

Eve Merriam (1916–92) was a poet, playwright, and lecturer who wrote several volumes of poetry and children's picture books.

Thomas Merton (1915–68) was a writer, poet, and priest best known for his autobiography, *The Seven Storey Mountain.*

Henry Miller (1891–1980) was an American author whose first two books, *Tropic of Cancer* and *Tropic of Capricorn*, were banned in the United States until the 1960s for obscenity.

John Milton (1608–74) was an English poet whose most famous work is the epic *Paradise Lost*.

Marianne Moore (1887–1972) was an American poet who won the 1951 Pulitzer Prize for her *Collected Poems*.

Robin Morgan is a poet, feminist, activist, and the former editor-in-chief of *Ms.* magazine.

Toni Morrison (1931–) won the 1977 National Book Award for her novel *Song of Solomon* and the 1987 Pulitzer Prize for *Beloved*. She received the Nobel Prize in Literature in 1993.

Mother Teresa of Calcutta (1910–97) was a Roman Catholic missionary in India and the recipient of the Nobel Peace Prize in 1979.

Karl E. Mundt (1900–74) was a U.S. congressman from South Dakota from 1939 to 1949 and a U.S. senator from 1949 to 1973.

John Middleton Murry (1889–1957), an English editor and author, was the editor of the *Rhythm* and *Athenaeum*.

A. J. Muste (Abraham Johannes Muste) (1885–1967) was a minister, pacifist, and Communist activist who helped found the Congress for Progressive Labor Action.

Jawaharlal Nehru (1889–1964) was president of the Indian National Congress political party and the first prime minister of independent India, serving from 1947 to 1964.

Pablo Neruda (1904–73) was a Chilean poet, Communist leader, and ambassador to France; he received the Nobel Prize in Literature in 1971.

Friedrich Wilhelm Nietzsche (1844–1900) was a German philosopher and moralist whose works include *The Birth of Tragedy*, *Thus Spake Zarathustra*, and *Beyond Good and Evil*.

Richard M. Nixon (Richard Milhouse Nixon) (1913–94) was the thirty-seventh president of the United States; in 1974, during his second term, he was forced to resign—the first U.S. president to do so—over his role in the Watergate affair.

Henri Nouwen (1932–96) was a Catholic priest, psychologist, and author who taught at Notre Dame University, Yale Divinity School, and Harvard University.

Kenzaburo Oe (1935–) is a Japanese novelist and essayists whose several books include *A Personal Matter* (1964). He was awarded the Nobel Prize in Literature in 1994.

Yoko Ono (1933–) is a musician and avante-garde performance artist who was married to John Lennon from 1969 until his death in 1980.

J. Robert Oppenheimer (1904–67), an American physicist, was director of the atomic-energy research project at Los Alamos, New Mexico. After the bombings of Japan, Oppenheimer became an advocate for international control of nuclear energy.

George Orwell (1903–50) was a British political novelist and essayist best known for his novels *Animal Farm* and *Nineteen Eighty-Four*.

Ovid (43 B.C.–A.D. 18) was a Latin poet whose major work is the *Metamorphoses*.

Blaise Pascal (1623–62) was a French scientist who turned to religious philosophy in 1654 after a near-death experience and conversion.

Boris Pasternak (1890–1960), a Russian poet, translator, and novelist, published *Doctor Zhivago* in 1957 despite its being banned in the USSR. He was awarded the 1958 Nobel Prize in Literature but, under pressure by the government, retracted his acceptance.

Katherine Paterson (1932–) is the author of several acclaimed children's books, including *Bridge to Terabithia* and *Jacob Have I Loved*.

George S. Patton, Jr. (1885–1945) was a major general in the U.S. Army during World War II.

Linus Pauling (1901–94), an American chemist and an advocate of world disarmament, received the Nobel Prize in Chemistry in 1954 and the Nobel Peace Prize in 1962.

Lester Pearson (1897–1972) was the prime minister of Canada from 1963 to 1968. As head of Canada's U.N. delegation, he had received the 1957 Nobel Peace Prize for his role in ending the 1956 Arab-Israeli war.

Petrarch (Francesco Petrarca) (1304–74) was a renowned Italian poet who was named laureate at Rome in 1348.

Peace Pilgrim (1908–81) was a pacifist who lectured nationwide at colleges, churches, and on television and radio.

Pope John Paul II (Karol Jozef Wojityla) (1920–) was elected pope of the Catholic Church in 1978; he is the first Polish pope.

Pope John XXIII (Angelo Giuseppe Roncalli) (1881–1963) was elected pope of the Catholic Church in 1958.

Pope Paul VI (Giovanni Battista Montini) (1897–1978) was elected pope of the Catholic Church in 1963.

Beilby Porteus (1731–1808) was a poet and chaplain whose most important work is the epic *Death: A Poetical Essay*.

François Rabelais (c. 1490–1553) was a French physician, writer, and monk.

Yitzhak Rabin (1922–95) was prime minister of Israel from 1974 to 1977 and from 1992 to 1995. He was jointly awarded the 1994 Nobel Peace Prize with Shimon Peres and Yasir Arafat, the leader of the Palestine Liberation Organization.

Jeannette Rankin (1880–1973) was a pacifist and the first female member of the U.S. Congress, serving first in 1917–19 and again in 1941–43.

Adrienne Rich (1929–) is an American poet who writes on feminist and lesbian themes; her many works of poetry and prose include *Diving into the Wreck* (1973), for which she won a National Book Award.

Mary Caroline Richards, a writer, educator, and poet, taught at the University of California at Berkeley, the University of Chicago, and Black Mountain College in North Carolina.

Hyman G. Rickover (1900–1986) was an admiral of the U.S. Navy from 1973 to 1981.

Mary Roberts Rinehart (1876–1958) was an American mystery writer, playwright, and the first female war correspondent in World War II, writing for the *Saturday Evening Post*.

Caryl Rivers is an essayist and a professor of journalism at Boston University.

Eleanor Roosevelt (1884–1962), the wife of U.S. president Franklin Delano Roosevelt, was a prominent social activist who wrote a syndicated newspaper column and served as U.S. delegate to the United Nations and as chair of the Commission on Human Rights.

Franklin Delano Roosevelt (1882–1945) was the thirty-second president of the United States, leading the country out of the Great Depression and into World War II. He died in office shortly after beginning an unprecedented fourth term.

Theodore Roosevelt (1858–1919), the twenty-sixth president of the United States, received the 1906 Nobel Peace Prize for his efforts to end the Russo-Japanese War. After leaving office, he criticized President Woodrow Wilson for his neutrality policy in World War I.

Muriel Rukeyser (1913–80) was an American poet whose first book of poetry, *Theory of Flight*, was published in 1935.

John Ruskin (1819–1900) was an English art critic and social theorist.

Bertrand Russell (1872–1970) was an English philosopher, mathematician, and pacifist who received the 1950 Nobel Prize in Literature.

Lord John Russell (1792–1878) was an earl and British Whig politician who served twice as prime minister of Great Britain.

Carl Sagan (1934–96) was a professor of astronomy at Cornell University, host of the television show *Cosmos*, and the author of the Pulitzer Prize–winning *The Dragons of Eden* and *Contact*.

Saint Francis of Assisi (c. 1182–1286), founder of the Franciscan order of friars, was said to love nature so much that he preached to the sparrows at Alviano. He was canonized by Pope Gregory IX in 1228.

Carl Sandburg (1878–1967) was an American poet, journalist, and biographer who won two Pulitzer prizes: one for his *Complete Poems* and the other for the last four volumes of his biography of Abraham Lincoln.

Oscar Arias Sánchez (1941–) was president of Costa Rica from 1986 to 1990. He was awarded the Nobel Peace Prize in 1987 for his regional peace initiative.

May Sarton (1912–95), an American poet, novelist, and memoirist, published fifty-three books, including *In Time Like Air* and *Journal of a Solitude*.

Jean-Paul Sartre (1905–80) was a leading French existentialist and Marxist, a playwright and novelist who was awarded–but declined–the Nobel Prize in Literature in 1964.

Maria Schell (1926–) is an Austrian actress who appeared in *The Last Bridge*, *White Nights*, and *End of Desire*.

Patricia Schroeder served as U.S. congresswoman from Colorado for twenty-four years, starting in 1972; she was the longest-serving woman in the history of Congress.

Martin Scorsese (1942–) is the director of the films *Mean Streets*, *Taxi Driver*, *Raging Bull*, *Goodfellas*, and *The Last Temptation of Christ*.

Roger Scruton is an English author and philosopher whose books include *England: An Elegy*.

William Shakespeare (1564–1616) was an English poet and playwright now renowned as one of literature's greatest figures.

George Bernard Shaw (1856–1950) was an Irish playwright and critic who wrote *Man and Superman*, *Androcles and the Lion*, and *Pygmalion*.

William Tecumseh Sherman (1820–91) was a Union general in the American Civil War, famous both for burning Atlanta and for marching to the sea, as well as for making the statement "War is all hell."

Beverly Sills (1929–) is an American opera singer who has been general director of the New York City Opera and chairwoman of Lincoln Center.

Socrates (469–399 B.C.) was a Greek philosopher who taught Plato; tried for religious heresy, he was sentenced to drink poisoned hemlock in 399 B.C.

Alexander Solzhenitsyn (1918–), a Russian writer, is the author of the novel *One Day in the Life of Ivan Denisovich*, which describes the labor camps to which he was sentenced for eight years. He was twice exiled for treason and was awarded the Nobel Prize in Literature in 1974.

Theodore C. Sorensen (1928–), a speechwriter and adviser to President John F. Kennedy, is the author of *Kennedy* and *Why I Am a Democrat*.

Herbert Spencer (1820–1903) was an English philosopher who worked successfully to promote acceptance of Darwin's theory of evolution.

Benedict Spinoza (1632–77) was a Dutch lens grinder and philosopher, most of whose work was published posthumously.

Freya Stark (1893–1993) was a travel writer and photographer; she wrote extensively about the Middle East and worked with the British government in World War II to win the Arab world to the Allied cause.

George Steiner (1929–) is a French-born critic and novelist whose books include *Errata: An Examined Life*.

Charles Sumner (1811–74) was a U.S. senator from Massachusetts from 1851 to 1874.

Publius Syrus (42 B.C.) came from Syrius and was sent to Rome as a slave, where he was eventually freed. Scholars believe that the collection of moral sayings bearing his name may not have been written solely by him.

Tacitus (Cornelius Tacitus) (c. 55–c. 117) was a Roman historian and orator.

Alfred Tennyson (1809–1892) was an English Victorian poet whose poems include "The Lotus-Eaters," "Ulysses," and "The Charge of the Light Brigade."

Margaret Thatcher (1925–) was the first woman prime minister of Great Britain, holding office (1979–90) longer than any other prime minister in the twentieth century.

Thomas à Kempis (1379–1471), a German monk at Mt. St. Agnes in the Netherlands, is known largely for his devotional work *The Imitation of Christ*.

Norman Thomas (1884–1968) was an American socialist leader and pacifist, the head of the Socialist Party, and an instrumental figure in establishing the American Civil Liberties Union.

Dorothy Thompson (1894–1961) was a foreign-affairs journalist and feminist who wrote for the *Philadelphia Public Ledger*, the *New York Evening Post*, and the *New York Herald Tribune*, where she was a political columnist.

Henry David Thoreau (1817–62), an American essayist and naturalist mentored by Ralph Waldo Emerson, wrote about his experience living in a small, isolated cabin on Walden Pond.

Christina Thürmer-Rohr is a German feminist who published *Vagabonding: Feminist Thinking Cut Loose*, a book of essays, in 1991.

Leo Tolstoy (1828–1910) was a Russian novelist, the author of *War and Peace* and *Anna Karenina*.

Arnold Toynbee (1852–83) was an English economist, historian, and social reformer who applied historical method to economic theory.

Harry S. Truman (1884–1972) was the thirty-third president of the United States, assuming office after the death of Franklin Delano Roosevelt in 1945. He was elected to a second term, which saw the outbreak of the Korean War.

Robert C. Tucker is professor emeritus of international studies at Princeton University and the former director of its Russian Studies program. His many books include *Stalin in Power* and *The Soviet Political Mind*.

Ted Turner (1938–), the founder of the Turner Broadcasting System (TBS), the Cable News Network (CNN), Turner Network Television (TNT), and the Cartoon Network, is vice chairman of AOL Time Warner.

Archbishop Desmond Tutu (1931–) was general secretary of the South African Council of Churches and the first black person to be elected archbishop of Cape Town. He was awarded the Nobel Peace Prize in 1984 for his campaign against apartheid.

Sun Tzu (c. 520–320 B.C.) is the name used by the unknown author or authors of *The Art of War*, the influential book of military strategy and philosophy.

Paul Valéry (1871–1945) was a French poet, critic, and essayist who served as president of the Committee of Letters and Arts of the League of Nations in the 1930s.

Gerard Vanderhaar is the author of several Christian books on nonviolence, including *Beyond Violence* and *Active Nonviolence*.

Bartolomeo Vanzetti (1888–1927), an Italian immigrant who settled in Massachusetts, was an anarchist and a co-defendant in the celebrated

Sacco-Vanzetti trial, in which he and Nicola Sacco were tried and convicted of murder on dubious evidence.

Vauvenargues (Marquis de Vauvenargues) (1715–47) was a French moralist.

Vegetius (Flavius Vegetius Renatus) (c. 385–400), a Roman, wrote about the Roman military system.

Frederick Vinson Moore (1890–1953) was chief justice of the U.S. Supreme Court from 1946 to 1953; prior to that, he was a longtime U.S. congressman and secretary of the Treasury.

Mary Heaton Vorse (1874–1966) was a journalist, novelist, suffragist, and labor activist who published a memoir, *A Footnote to Folly*.

Marilyn Vos Savant, listed in the *Guinness Book of World Records* as having the world's highest recorded IQ (228), has written several books and pens *Parade* magazine's "Ask Marilyn" column.

Jim Wallis, a preacher, newspaper columnist, and political activist, is the editor-in-chief of *Sojourners* magazine and founder of Call to Renewal, a federation of faith-based organizations fighting poverty.

Booker T. Washington (1856–1915) founded the prestigious Tuskegee Institute in Atlanta, which became one of the premier centers of learning for African-Americans. He also wrote several books, among them his autobiography, *Up From Slavery*.

George Washington (1732–99) was the first president of the United States, serving from 1789 to 1797.

H. G. Wells (Herbert George Wells) (1866–1946) is best known for his science-fiction novels, including *The Time Machine*, *The Invisible Man*, and *The War of the Worlds*.

Orson Welles (1915–85) co-wrote, produced, directed, and starred in *Citizen Kane*, winning an Academy Award for the screenplay. In addition to his numerous other films, he is famed for his radio broadcast of H. G. Welles's *The War of the Worlds*, which led panicked listeners to believe they were under attack by Martians.

Rebecca West (Cicely Isabel Fairfield) (1892–1983) was a British journalist whose most famous book is *Black Lamb and Grey Falcon*, which was based on her observations in Yugoslavia. She was made a Dame Commander, Order of the British Empire, in 1959.

E. B. White (Elwyn Brooks White) (1899–1995) wrote "Talk of the Town" for *The New Yorker*, revised William Strunk, Jr.'s *The Elements of Style*, and was the author of *Stuart Little* and *Charlotte's Web*.

Alfred North Whitehead (1861–1947), a mathematician and philosopher, wrote *Principia Mathematica* with Bertrand Russell as well as several books of his own. He taught at Trinity College in Cambridge, the University of London, and Harvard University.

Walt Whitman (1819–92), an American poet, is best known for *Leaves of Grass*, which he first published in 1855 and continued to revise throughout his life.

John Greenleaf Whittier (1807–92) was a Quaker poet, politician, and abolitionist who wrote frequently on New England farm and village life.

Elie Wiesel (1928–), who was born in Romania, was sent to Nazi concentration camps at the age of sixteen; now a U.S. citizen, he has written numerous novels and memoirs about the Holocaust and received the Nobel Peace Prize in 1986.

Oscar Wilde (1854–1900), an Irish writer and a celebrated wit, wrote *The Picture of Dorian Gray, An Ideal Husband,* and *The Importance of Being Earnest.* In 1895, he was tried and sentenced to two years in prison for his relationship with Lord Alfred Douglas.

Thornton Wilder (1897–1975) was an American playwright and novelist who won a Pulitzer Prize for his novel *The Bridge of San Luis Rey* and two more for his plays *Our Town* and *The Skin of Our Teeth.* He was awarded the first National Medal for Literature in 1965.

Woodrow Wilson (1856–1924) was the twenty-eighth president of the United States, serving from 1913 to 1921. His efforts to remain neutral in World War I earned him reelection; after the United States entered the war, Wilson negotiated the Treaty of Versailles with European leaders in Paris.

Harriet Woods (1927–) was the lieutenant governor of Missouri from 1985 to 1989 and is the author of *Stepping Up to Power: The Political Journey of American Women*.

Virginia Woolf (1882–1941), an English novelist and essayist and a member of the Bloomsbury group of artists and writers, was the author of *Mrs. Dalloway*, *A Room of One's Own*, and many other books.

Malcolm X (1925–1965) was a militant African-American leader and Muslim minister who broke from the Black Muslims to form the rival Muslim Mosque, Inc.

Bibliography

Andrews, Robert, ed. *The Columbia Dictionary of Quotations*. New York: Columbia University Press, 1993.

Andrews, Robert; Mary Biggs, and Michael Seidel, eds. *The Columbia World of Quotations*. New York: Columbia University Press, 1996.

Bartlett, John. *Familiar Quotations, 10th edition*. Boston: Little, Brown and Company, 1919.

Bartlett, John, and Justin Kaplan, general editor. *Familiar Quotations, sixteenth edition*. Boston: Little, Brown and Company, 1992.

Cohen, M. J. *The Penguin Thesaurus of Quotations*. New York: Penguin Books, 2000.

Ehrlich, Eugene, and Marshall DeBruhl, eds. *The International Thesaurus of Quotations*. New York: HarperPerennial, 1996.

Frank, Leonard Roy. *Random House Webster's Quotationary*. New York: Random House, 1999.

Jones, Alison, ed. *Chambers Dictionary of Quotations*. New York: Chambers, 1999.

Knowles, Elizabeth. *The Oxford Dictionary of Phrase, Saying, and Quotation*. New York: Oxford University Press, 1997.

Maggio, Rosalie, ed. *New Beacon Book of Quotations By Women*. Boston: Beacon Press, 1996.

Mieder, Wolfgang, ed. *Proverbs from Around the World*. Paramus, NJ: Prentice Hall, 1998.

Partnow, Elaine T., ed. *The Quotable Woman*. New York: Checkmark Books, 2001.

Simpson, James Beasley, comp. *Simpson's Contemporary Quotations*. Boston: Houghton Mifflin Company, 1988.

Thomsett, Michael C., and Jean Freestone Thomsett, eds. *War and Conflict Quotations*. Jefferson, NC: McFarland & Co., 1997.

Index